William B. Bjornstad
December 22, 1964

BAROQUE LYRIC POETRY

LOWRY NELSON, JR.

BAROQUE LYRIC POETRY

New Haven and London

YALE UNIVERSITY PRESS

Preface

In literary history, as elsewhere, every generalization is an hypothesis to be tested. It is in the spirit of speculative inquiry that I offer certain generalizations concerning Baroque poetic style. My point of departure is the poetry itself, and not preconceptions about the "spirit of the age" or the views of other critics. If I leave out of my account any consideration of the arguments of, for example, Rosemond Tuve or Odette de Mourgues, it is because their concern is mostly with imagery and world-view; my stress lies on other elements of poetry, and anyway I am skeptical about their conclusions. If, in general, I have slighted important views put forth concerning Baroque poetry, it is, I think, in most cases out of choice rather than ignorance. My intention is to exemplify rather than to exhaust.

Certain questions must go begging in any treatise. I have, for instance, attempted no rigorous definition of the lyric. Very little of the great poetry of the Baroque age was written to be sung; hence a restrictive definition would serve no purpose. Some of the poetry I deal with could perhaps be called narrative, though hardly in the sense one would use

the word to describe the *Orlando furioso* or *Paradise Lost* or
even *Hero and Leander* or *L'Adone*. Further, I have for the
most part assumed that the poems to which I give greatest
stress are aesthetically great. Criteria of greatness such as
complexity, unity, and adequate relation to reality would
have to be argued elsewhere. In other words, though any
critic must "judge," I have minimized evaluation in favor of
analysis.

Some apology should be offered, perhaps, for the ungainly
terms "dramaticality" and "manipulatable." It is strange that
English has no comfortable word to signify the effect of
dramatic skill. "Theatricality," often singled out as a Baroque
characteristic, seems to carry too overtly pejorative a meaning. Alternative possibilities, such as "dramaticity" and "dra-
maticism," ring even more dully on the ear. As for "manipulatable," it may indulgently be considered shorthand for a
periphrasis.

My main conclusions were set forth in a dissertation sub-
mitted to Yale University in 1951. Since then I have confirmed them in my own mind and modified them, I hope to
advantage, in their present form. Along the way I have
profited from the close and critical perusal of Renato Pog-
gioli (who read the first part) and Harry Levin (who read
the second). Their encouragements and reservations have
helped me to confirm my own views. I wish also to thank
Jonas Barish and Elias Mengel for their friendly help. It is
mostly because I had an expectant reader in René Wellek that
the work was done at all.

Among generous institutions, my hearty thanks are due
the Society of Fellows (Harvard); the Ford Foundation,
which has supported publication; and the Yale University
Press, whose expertness is for me most vividly personified
in my friend David Horne.

L. N., Jr.

New Haven
March 1960

Contents

I. BAROQUE: WORD AND CONCEPT

In its brief career as a critical term the word "baroque" has suffered extremes of interpretation. For some it is a universal aspect of human nature, and for others it is limited both in time and extent. It has been given somber connotations of vice and extravagance, but also lustrous connotations of devotion and austerity. Variously it has been linked with florescence, maturity, and decay. Some would claim it for the visual arts alone; others would enlarge its scope to include all the arts; and still others would stretch it even farther to describe a quality of mind. If all the voices raised were to sing together, they could only produce cacophony. In the midst of such confusion, one way to begin establishing order is to examine the word's credentials.

In the past "baroque" was thought to derive from the Portuguese and Spanish *barroco,* an irregular pearl or a promontory, which in turn was said to derive from the Latin *verruca,* meaning a wart or an incline; and some still hold to that explanation, though without very sound linguistic evidence. Recently it has been convincingly derived from *baroco,* a term used by the Schoolmen to describe a kind of syllogism. This derivation has the advantage of historical support, both linguistic and semantic. Tracing the word back as far as it goes, we come finally to William of Shyreswood, who revived Aristotelian logic in the earlier thirteenth century.[1] It was

1. Described by Roger Bacon as "longe sapientior Alberto [Magno]," William of Shyreswood (died after 1267) had been known to logicians through

3

he who seems to have invented the "words" contained in the
mnemonic hexameters:

> Barbara celarent darii ferio baralipton
> Celantes dabitis fapesmo frisesomorum
> Cesare campestres festino baroco darapti
> Felapton disamis datisi bocardo ferison.

Each "word" is a code description of a syllogistic mood. The
letters of which they are composed signify the conditions of a
syllogism: *a* means a universal affirmative proposition; *e* a
universal negative; *i* a particular affirmative; *o* a particular
negative; *s, p, m,* and *b* in company with *r* indicate the opera-
tions by which the syllogism can be converted to the first or
"perfect" figure. According to the scheme invented by Aris-
totle and perpetuated in the Middle Ages, *baroco* represents
the fourth mood of the second figure, consisting of a major

---

the work of Carl Prantl (*Geschichte der Logik im Abendlande*, Leipzig,
1855–70, *3*, 15–16) as the propagator of the mnemonic verses. We now have
authoritative testimony to William's originality as their inventor. In his
"Einleitung" to the first printing of the *Introductiones in logicam des Wil-
helm von Shyreswood*, Sitzungsberichte der bayerischen Akademie der Wis-
senschaften, Philosophisch-historischen Abteilung, Heft 10 (Munich, 1937), p.
27, Martin Grabmann states: "Die bekannten Memorialverse . . . habe ich
in diesen älteren Logiklehrbüchern [treatises still in ms. which antedate
William] nicht gefunden." We may then presume that Petrus Hispanus got
the verses from William, who was allegedly his teacher, and that he popu-
larized them through his immensely successful *Summulae logicales*. The
early history of the word can be traced by putting together the citations
from writers like St. Bernardine, Vives, Erasmus, Montaigne, Ferrari, Sol-
dani, Saint-Simon, which are found in Littré's *Dictionnaire*, the *New English Dictionary*, and the following books and articles: Karl Borinski, *Die
Antike in Poetik und Kunsttheorie* (Leipzig, 1914), *1*, 199, 308; Benedetto
Croce, *Storia dell'età barocca in Italia* (Bari, 1929), pp. 20–23; Gustav Schnu-
rer, *Katholische Kirche und Kultur in der Barockzeit* (Paderborn, 1937),
p. 68; Carlo Calcaterra, "Il problema del barocco," *Problemi ed orientamenti
critici di lingua e di letteratura italiana*, ed. Attilio Momigliano (Milan,
1949), pp. 405–501; Georg Weise, "Considerazioni di storia dell'arte intorno
al barocco," *Rivista di letterature moderne, 3* (1952), 5–14.

premise that is universal and affirmative and a minor premise that is particular and negative, yielding a conclusion that is particular and negative. William of Shyreswood furnishes his own oddly coincidental example: every pearl is a stone; some men are not stones; therefore some men are not pearls. For our purposes it is important to note that the word *baroco* was pure artifice and that, through practically all later logic books in the Middle Ages and Renaissance it became part of every schoolboy's mnemonic grab bag. By Montaigne and by certain Italian satirists of the sixteenth century, to mention only those instances, *baroco* was singled out, often with *baralipton,* as an egregious kind of hairsplitting or double talk. It little matters why those words should become the proverbial ones, whether by random selection or by reason of their explosive sounds: we are most concerned with the fact that *baroco* survived the longest and, leaving behind its artificial and homely origin, entered a new and exotic life. Thus we may hope to dispel the naive hope that the origin of the word may tell us what it now means.

The later history of "baroque" is more obvious. By the end of the eighteenth century the term was associated particularly with architecture and means something like "bizarre" or "extravagant." Jacob Burckhardt gave it historical limits when he used it to describe the style of architecture that developed out of the "decay" of the High Renaissance. But Heinrich Wölfflin in 1888 seems to have been the first to suggest a favorable approach to Baroque architecture. In doing so he freed the term from necessarily pejorative connotations and recommended that it be applied also to the other arts. Since then, and especially since the appearance of Wölfflin's *Kunstgeschichtliche Grundbegriffe* in 1915, Baroque has become standard in art history as a period concept refined now to the point of designating the style that prevailed in Western Europe between Mannerism and Rococo. In the course of its semantic mutations, Baroque had lost any significant con-

nection with its origin and had become a convenient label
for a style whose merits and continuity could be argued apart
from any hostile prejudice.[2]

In literary scholarship it was a long time before any need
was felt for a comprehensive term to designate the style between Renaissance and Neoclassicism. In Spain and France
the honorific word "classic" was applied to the drama, considered the main glory of the literature of the time. As for
lyric poetry, it was customary to think of Malherbe and
Boileau as "classic" and Góngora and Quevedo as, respec-
tively, *cultista* and *conceptista*. Until recently Spanish literary historians were usually content to join eighteenth-
century critics in condemning *cultismo* and *conceptismo* as
mere vice-ridden decadence.[3] In Italy, since there were no
great playwrights or novelists to consider, literary historians
had to acknowledge the central importance of Marino. The
terms *marinismo* and *secentismo* were in current use in the
nineteenth century as designations for the dominant style. In
Germany, though many Baroque texts were edited and published during the middle and late nineteenth century, not
much critical attention was given the period until the
word Baroque came to be widely used in art history. It
found less competition with traditional terms, such as
Schwulst, than in other countries. England, perhaps more
than France, has put up the strongest resistance to the concept of Baroque. England's literary Renaissance was rather
belated and in many ways episodic. The first major phase
seemed to coincide more or less with the reign of Henry VIII

2. For an account of the later uses of "Baroque" and a thorough discussion of its relevance to literary historiography, see René Wellek, "The Concept of the Baroque in Literary Scholarship," *Journal of Aesthetics and Art
Criticism,* 5 (1946), 77–109. There full references are given, together with a
chronological bibliography of works that mention Baroque in connection
with literature. My account proceeds from his.

3. The tercentenary commemoration of Góngora's death in 1927 was the
occasion for several important critical editions and essays; in effect, the beginnings of a general reappraisal of Spanish Baroque poetry.

and the second with that of Elizabeth; it was therefore convenient to give them political labels. Since Elizabeth happened to die about the time a great change in style was taking place, the following period could be dubbed Jacobean after the succeeding monarch. But the matter was somewhat confused by the political intrusion of the Puritan Revolution and later by the Restoration. Certainly it is not elucidated by protracting the Renaissance to the death of Milton (1674) or beginning the age of Neoclassicism with Denham's *Cooper's Hill* (1642).

At present the concept of Baroque seems to be domesticated in Italy, mainly through the efforts of Croce, and in Germany, as a result of the concentrated labors of a number of literary historians oriented in *Geistesgeschichte*.[4] Likewise among historians of Spanish literature it has gained general acceptance.[5] But in English and French literary scholarship there is still considerable opposition to its use. Critics such as Henri Peyre and Fernand Baldensperger have argued against accepting Baroque as a period concept in French literature.[6] At the same time others have adopted the term, especially to designate what is loosely called *poésie précieuse*.[7] Still others, Leo Spitzer and Helmut Hatzfeld, would go much further and apply it to the whole period.[8] In English literary scholar-

4. Notably Fritz Strich, Karl Viëtor, and Helmut Hatzfeld, as well as Herbert Cysarz (Austrian) and Theophil Spoerri (Swiss).

5. For example, Dámaso Alonso, Ángel Valbuena Prat, and Américo Castro.

6. See Peyre's *Le Classicisme française* (New York, 1942), pp. 181–83; and Baldensperger's "Pour une Révaluation littéraire du XVIIe siècle classique," *Revue d'histoire littéraire de la France, 44* (1937), 1–15.

7. See, for example, the Baroque number of the *Revue des sciences humaines* (Lille), new ser. *55–56,* 1949; and the *Cahiers de l'Association Internationale des Etudes Françaises, 1,* 1951.

8. Leo Spitzer, "Die klassische Dämpfung in Racines Stil," in *Romanische Stil- und Literaturstudien* (Marburg, 1931), *1,* 135–268; and "The 'Récit de Théramène,'" chapter 3 of *Linguistics and Literary History* (Princeton, 1948), pp. 87–134. Helmut Hatzfeld, "Die französische Klassik in neuer

ship, despite the great interest in the seventeenth century, Baroque has not yet won approval. There is, all the same, a growing curiosity about it; and perhaps in time that curiosity, together with the more conservative tendency under way to minimize the stark old contrast between Elizabethan and Jacobean and the recent movement to "reconcile" Donne and Milton, will lead to the formulation of a period concept which might just as well be called Baroque.[9]

When one considers the newness of the literary concept and its variable fortunes at the hands of critics and historians, one can hardly be surprised that little of the great quantity of scholarship devoted to Baroque is directly concerned with literary style and that still less is concerned with characterizing literary style in an historically bounded period between Renaissance and Neoclassicism. Most theorizing about Baroque has centered on the visual arts or has attempted to comprise the whole expanse of cultural history. As a way of defining the essence of Baroque, its origin or moving force has been ascribed variously to psychology and to history. There are those like Eugenio d'Ors who consider Baroque a recurrent phenomenon, not limited to one historical period.[10] Even some historians of literature follow the same trend of thought: Ernst Robert Curtius, for example, is prone to do so.[11] But the majority of cultural and art historians are, fortunately, content to view Baroque as a style limited in time. Of the several historical "explanations" of Baroque, perhaps the most persistent is that which links it with the

Sicht: Klassik als Barock," *Tijdschrift voor Taal en Letteren*, *23* (1935), 213–81.

9. See, for instance, F. P. Wilson, *Elizabethan and Jacobean*, Oxford, 1945; Douglas Bush, *English Literature in the Earlier Seventeenth Century*, Oxford, 1945 (especially pp. 1–4); and Rosemond Tuve, *Elizabethan and Metaphysical Imagery*, Chicago, 1947.

10. In his book *Du Baroque*, Paris, 1935.

11. See "Manierismus," chapter 15 of *Europäische Literatur und lateinisches Mittelalter*, Bern, 1948; English version, New York, 1953.

Counter Reformation.[12] It is true that much of Baroque art was religious and much poetry of the time was devotional (to use the customary terms); but they were not all Roman Catholic and certainly not all sponsored by the Jesuits. When one considers the great poetry of the time as a whole, one must allow that it was both devotional and secular, both Catholic and Protestant. Attempts have been made to embrace the "extremes," and epitomize Baroque in the tension generated by the compresence of sensualism and spirituality,[13] or naturalism and illusionism.[14] Bernini's St. Teresa is usually mentioned, and one could also think of the customary Baroque dome paintings that depict the sky with clouds and angels. Another attempt to characterize Baroque has been made in terms of social history. Baroque style is said by some to be "courtly." [15] But that hardly distinguishes it adequately from Renaissance style, nor does it cope with the powerful influences of the forever rising bourgeoisie.

Where, then, are we left? No "explanation" seems able to take into account all phases of life during the period. No characterization of style seems adequate to all the arts. Surely it is time to reconsider the bases for generalization. From a theoretical point of view many crucial difficulties have been bypassed or ignored. It is assumed too easily that criteria of style from one art can be taken over and applied to another. Certainly the relatively successful example of Wölfflin in dealing with the visual arts calls for emulation. But it is questionable whether his categories can be directly applied to

12. For example, Werner Weisbach, *Der Barock als Kunst der Gegenreformation*, Berlin, 1921; Paul Hankamer, *Deutsche Gegenreformation und deutscher Barock*, Stuttgart, 1935.
13. For example, W. P. Friederich, *Spiritualismus und Sensualismus in der englischen Barocklyrik*, Vienna, 1932; and Weisbach.
14. For example: Ludwig Pfandl, *Geschichte der spanischen Nationalliteratur in ihrer Blütezeit*, Freiburg im Breisgau, 1929.
15. See Günther Müller, "Höfische Kultur der Barockzeit," in Hans Naumann and Günther Müller's *Höfische Kultur*, Halle, 1929.

literature, and also whether any mere modification of them would touch central problems in the history of literary style.[16] Unargued analogies between the arts can lead only to vague subjective impressions of similarity. All the same, Wölfflin's categories may suggest purely literary criteria, concerned, in the case of poetry, with poetic structure. Just as Wölfflin dealt with the totality of the work of art, so the critic of literature should deal with the totality of the literary work. The example of method is admirable; but it is the method, not the actual categories, which should be imitated. Another theoretical difficulty often overlooked is the relation between the work of art and social or intellectual history. In the Baroque age it is especially difficult to define any coherent *Zeitgeist* which would account for the philosophy of Descartes and Hobbes, the Counter Reformation, and libertinage and pietism, and which would remain at the same time distinct from the *Zeitgeist* of the Renaissance. To stop short of a *Zeitgeist* and identify Baroque poetic style with any one aspect of intellectual life would be to limit it arbitrarily. It might be permissible to deduce the world-view of a lyric and relate it to some philosophical or social trend, but it is doubtful that we would learn much about poetic style. So often ideas in poetry, when reduced by philosophical analysis and deprived of their emotive or aesthetic significance, become universal commonplaces; and as such they can hardly be characterized historically. Rather than attempt to decoct ideas from poetry, the critic-historian should see how they react in solution. Poetically their meaning is largely determined by their mode of presentation. Considering, then, the welter of impression-

16. Examples of fairly literal applications of Wölfflin's categories are to be found Theophil Spoerri's *Renaissance und Barock bei Ariost und Tasso: Versuch einer Anwendung Wölfflin'scher Kunstbetrachtung*, Bern, 1922; Darnell Roaten and F. Sánchez y Escribano's *Wölfflin's Principles in Spanish Drama: 1500–1700*, New York, 1952; and Wylie Sypher's *Four Stages of Renaissance Style: Transformations in Art and Literature, 1400–1700*, Garden City, N.Y., 1955.

istic analogies and theoretical confusions, it would seem sensible to begin with purely literary criteria of a general sort and discover what their application to Baroque poetry reveals.
A great deal of effort has been expended on Baroque poetic style, whether under that or some other name. Most of it has concerned imagery and metaphor and rhetorical figures. Traditionally the style of Marino, Góngora, and Donne is characterized by their use of the "conceit" or the far-fetched metaphor. In Italy and Spain the "conceited" style was early described and codified by Emanuele Tesauro and Baltasar Gracián, not to mention others of less importance.[17] And in England the "Metaphysicals" were early named by Dryden and Dr. Johnson,[18] and characterized as employing extravagant metaphors fashioned from the linkage of disparates. Most later criticism has followed the same approach. Recent critics have not paid sufficient attention to Marino's style; but Góngora's has been analyzed in great detail, mainly by Dámaso Alonso, who has painstakingly codified and defended Gongorine syntax and metaphor.[19] Donne's use of metaphor has been frequently discussed: it has even been claimed that his most characteristic poems derive their structure from a single metaphor extended throughout.[20] But there are serious objections to defining Baroque poetic style in terms of the "conceit" and other rhetorical figures. Were they not extensively used in other periods? In particular, do they not derive from the Middle Ages and the Petrarchan tradition? The repertory of medieval *topoi* Curtius has collected should

17. Tesauro in *Cannocchiale aristotelico* (1654) and Gracián in *Arte de ingenio* (1642), later revised as *Agudeza y arte de ingenio* (1648).

18. Dryden in his *Essay on Satire* (1693) and Johnson in his *Life of Cowley* (1779).

19. *Evolución de la sintaxis de Góngora*, Madrid, 1928; *La lengua poética de Góngora*, Madrid, 1928; *Estudios y ensayos gongorinos*, Madrid, 1955.

20. See Leonard Unger's critique of the "metaphorical" approach in *Donne's Poetry and Modern Criticim*, Chicago, 1950; now reprinted in the author's collection *The Man in the Name*, Minneapolis, 1956.

caution literary historians to reconsider the originality of the Baroque "conceit." [21] And the well-known existence of an anti-Petrarchan movement in the Baroque should encourage attempts to distinguish, if possible, between Petrarchan and Baroque "conceits," according to the way they are actually used in context. At the present time studies in metaphor are usually limited to one literature and often to one poet or poem. Eventually they should provide a basis for generalization; even now probably a great deal could be learned if the subject were treated more broadly and boldly. No doubt most of what has been written about the Baroque "conceit" has some foundation, some relevance, to the poems in which it is found. But to measure the achievement of the Baroque poets and to characterize their style it is necessary to proceed historically as well as critically, taking into account the whole European tradition. The question of direct influences and borrowings is an important one, though not conclusive; for the relationship between "emitter" and "receptor" is often more oblique than mere verbal parallels would suggest. Much more important, and historically more conclusive, are the similarities among national traditions in the way metaphor is used as an element of structure.

Apart from studies in metaphor, what has been done to define Baroque poetic style? In German literary scholarship, for example, attempts to define it have often been vitiated by extraliterary assumptions, such as ready-made theories of the origins of the Baroque *Geist* or mechanical transpositions of criteria from art to literature. On these grounds we can arraign the work of Herbert Cysarz and, to a lesser degree, of Theophil Spoerri and Fritz Strich. [22] Some of their findings,

21. *Europäische Literatur und lateinisches Mittelalter*, Bern, 1948; English version, New York, 1953.

22. Cysarz, *Deutsches Barock in der Lyrik*, Leipzig, 1936; Spoerri, *Renaissance und Barock bei Ariost und Tasso*, Bern, 1922; Strich, "Der lyrische Stil des 17. Jahrhunderts," *Abhandlungen zur deutschen Literaturgeschichte: Festschrift für Franz Muncker* (Munich, 1916), pp. 21–53.

however, are valuable for the history of style. Strich, for instance, is certainly justified in making a great deal of asyndeton in German Baroque poetry; but his conclusions need the refinement and historical support which Karl Viëtor suggests in his critique.[23] In general terms, it may appear that one or a number of rhetorical figures are peculiar to Baroque, yet examples can usually be adduced from other periods: the readiest way out of the impasse is to discover how rhetorical figures work within the total poem or, in other words, to define their use as means of poetic structure. One attempt to go beyond rhetorical figures is Helmut Hatzfeld's analysis of the religious "classical" lyric in France from which he derives characteristic motives or themes.[24] Several of them, "überraschende Gedankenverschlingung," "Schleierantithese," "intensive Überladung durch Wortwiederholung und Worthäufung," have been used before in describing Baroque poetic style; but others—the contrast between "moi seul" and "tout l'univers" (the "seul-tout-Formel"), "Glanz-und Morbidezza-Motive"—suggest new departures. More recently, and in regard to French literature, Imbrie Buffum has in his various studies attempted to induce categories of Baroque style which adequately regard both detail and world-view.[25] In D'Aubigné he sees exemplification of "forcefulness," "theatricality," "mutability," and other qualities which, when taken together, stamp his style as Baroque. In Jean de La Ceppède and in Saint-Amant he finds also "theatricality," "emphasis and exaggeration," "horror," "contrast and sur-

23. Karl Viëtor, *Probleme der deutschen Barockliteratur* (Leipzig, 1928), especially pp. 1–7.

24. "Der Barockstil der religiösen klassischen Lyrik in Frankreich," *Literaturwissenschaftliches Jahrbuch der Görresgesellschaft, 4* (1929), 30–60. See also his *Literature through Art: A New Approach to French Literature* (New York, 1952), in which he proposes further categories—for example, renunciation, resignation, and boundlessness.

25. *Agrippa d'Aubigné's "Les Tragiques": A Study of the Baroque Style in Poetry*, New Haven, 1951; and *Studies in the Baroque from Montaigne to Rotrou*, New Haven, 1957.

prise," to mention only those. Just as suggestive, if not conclusive, are the categories of Jean Rousset.[26] He generalizes that French literature of the seventeenth century runs from "instability" through "mobility" and "metamorphosis" (all symbolized by Circe and Proteus) to what he calls the "domination du décor" (symbolized by the peacock). But here, despite fresh insights and new material on the court masque, we begin to lose touch with the actual works of literary art. The basic problem in elaborating sets of categories seems to be the difficulty of hitting on the most significant and characterizing level of generalization.

The process of isolating characteristic features, relating them to poetic structure, and defining the style of a period cannot but entail the gradual discovery of a world-view. From social and cultural history one may gather hints and guesses; there is always the danger, however, that they become idées fixes or molds into which poems are forced to fit. Radical polarities, naturalism and illusionism, this-worldliness and other-worldliness, sensualism and spirituality, used by some to comprehend Baroque literary style, need not lead us to believe that the style is incoherent or its origins impossibly manifold. Indeed, they may in the end help us to see that the complexities of existence were more conscientiously, if not more conclusively, represented in the Baroque than in the Renaissance lyric. It might be shown that the "polarities," time and eternity, the physical and the spiritual, the microcosm and the macrocosm, produced tensions, not doctrinally resolved, which had gone unexploited in previous poetry; and that, in order to cope with their complexities and also with the intricacies of human relations, each polarity was expressed in such a way as to take its opposite into account. In other words, the expression of a "unified sensibility" in Baroque literature may actually reflect an uneasy and mo-

26. La Littérature de l'âge baroque en France, Circé et le paon, Paris, 1953. Another set of suggestive categories is to be found in Alexandre Cioranescu's El barroco, o el descubrimiento del drama, La Laguna, 1957.

mentary balancing of disparates, corresponding to the *concordia discors* of the "conceit." All this might be put under the heading of the poem's relation to reality, which any literary criticism that aspires to completeness must eventually face: it is of course finally impossible to isolate elements of style from the world-view of a poem. But the first step in any analysis is to understand the poem in itself, as far as that is possible; then one is in a position to relate it to reality and to other poems, other tendencies, and other styles. The process of understanding a poem begins with an analysis that carefully dissects the elements of style and reveals their interconnections and also their relation to the total structure. There is no need for the critic to put the poem back together again, since in its literary reality it can never be dismembered: once the poem's characteristics are understood, they can be compared to those of other poems, and the foundation is laid for a history of style. It is only in the later stages of stylistic analysis that one may begin to speak of a world-view, for the poem must first be understood as an immediate communication.

It is reasonable to suppose tentatively that some "essential" development in style took place between the Renaissance and the age of Neoclassicism. To define it does not mean that every poem written in the period must, therefore, be described in terms of dominant and original trends. We must call the putative style something, and the term nearest at hand is Baroque; indeed we could hardly impose any other. But it must be understood as *literary* Baroque, without irrelevant commitments from its use in the other arts and without any necessarily pejorative connotations.

In the realm of stylistic analysis many studies have been made of language, imagery, and metaphor in Baroque poets. Individual poems have been explicated and individual styles characterized. In particular, close attention has centered on Donne and the Metaphysicals, German religious poets, and Góngora. But usually those studies do not build

from the poem to the individual style and finally to the style
of the age. Their scope is limited and the implications of
their findings are not clearly shown. Since so much has been
written on Baroque language and imagery, especially "conceit" and metaphor, and since the question of fixing them
historically is so vexed, I have decided to adopt other approaches which have been neglected and which may provide
at least as sure a way of characterizing Baroque style. There
is some novelty in the broad scope of my study. Poems from
five national traditions are discussed, under the assumption
that linguistic differences can be minimized and that a general European Baroque style may be at least posited. At the
same time I have not considered the usual question of influences in any way decisive. To know, for example, that
Drummond of Hawthornden or Hofmannswaldau translated
minor poems of Marino does not add much to our understanding of the dominant style of the age as it was practiced
by the major poets. In any event, the history of influences
and fortunes is nowhere near complete; what conclusions can
be drawn from it will have to wait. I do not mean to imply
that national traditions and international influences may be
argued out of existence; but the former must be seen in terms
of the general movement and the latter must not be limited
to the mere fact of translation or verbal parallels. The scope
of my study, then, includes the major European national
traditions. It is well to insist upon relating elements of style
to total structure. Too often studies in imagery and syntax
leave undetermined the relation of those elements to the
whole poem; too often they become pseudo-scientific cata-
logues or extraliterary debates. The only sure way ever to
characterize a style historically is to begin by analyzing salient
features of a poem and show how they are related to the
main structure.

The chief novelty of this study lies perhaps in the stylistic
categories, time and drama, by which it proceeds. Every poem

depends in some measure upon time and drama.[27] Even contemporary verbless poems have an implied tense. And even imageless poems have an implied "dramatic" or "rhetorical" situation. But time and drama are not always made conspicuous or important sources of structure. To my mind they were first made so in the Baroque age, and for that reason their use should certainly enter into a characterization of Baroque poetic style. I shall consider a number of "good" poems from the point of view first of time structure and then of dramatic or rhetorical structure, with two main purposes in mind: to determine the structure of the individual poems and then to show similarities between them which help to characterize their common style.

27. Used in connection with lyric poetry, the word "drama" needs definition. Briefly, I take it to mean the full use of the "rhetorical members" (speaker, audience, reader) or, more generally, the "rhetorical situation" of a poem. Most often I speak of the effect achieved as "dramaticality." All these terms will later be defined both explicitly and in practice.

II. TIME AS A MEANS OF STRUCTURE

1. The Uses of Time in Poetry

It would be indeed rash to claim a wholly new poetic practice for the Baroque age, since the Baroque age is the child of the Renaissance and the Renaissance, as so many have labored to show, is the child of the Middle Ages. Besides, the classical tradition continued from Antiquity to persist in one form or another. We should look for changes only in accident, then, and not in substance. Family resemblances constantly arise and make it difficult to distinguish significant change. As far as outward form is concerned, the Baroque age hardly invented anything new: the sonnet and many lyric stanzas came ultimately from medieval "Romania" and the ode and heroic epistle, to mention only those, came from classical Antiquity; and they were all inherited directly from the Renaissance. Nonetheless, in the style of poetry there occurred a change which can be partially characterized in terms of tense or time. One is tempted at this point to turn to the speculative writers of the age (Montaigne, Bruno, Descartes, Galileo, Bacon) or to the religious writers (Boehme, the Cambridge Platonists, Pascal) in an effort to muster explicit "documentation"; and it is true that among them we may find illuminating texts. Yet it is a mistake to rely solely upon expository writers for our comprehension of a period. So often they merely rework old notions and so often they omit their hidden assumptions. The relation between pure literature and expository writing is often more oblique than we like to admit. Let it suffice for the present, then, to say in gross terms that the Middle Ages had a Christian idea of time as ordained by God and therefore "objective" and, except by God's will, immutable. We may say in general that the Renaissance did little directly to upset the medieval idea of time. It was only later that the *temporal* implications of Renaissance rebellion against orthodox philosophy and physics were realized. But we are not obliged to heel to the expressed thoughts of contemporary writers. It is just as valid and more revealing to proceed empirically over the field of pure literature and chiefly over the plot of lyric poetry.

In characterizing an historical period it is not often unique traits but rather unique configurations of traits that one can significantly analyze; in other words, one can only hope to deal accurately in tints rather than primary colors. With this in mind I shall try to show, first, that in certain Baroque poems there is a heightened awareness of time and, second, that the awareness can be seen in important instances as structural patterns of tense. Only after an accumulation of evidence will I draw conclusions. Some examples, true enough, could be matched by poems from earlier ages and many Baroque poems show none of the traits I wish to describe. It is a matter of sifting and weighing. Since it would not only be tedious but also impracticable to catalogue all Renaissance poetry, the reader is invited to draw upon his acquaintance with earlier lyrics so that he may test the evidence.

Since poems to be perceived must be read or, better, "performed," in some way they depend upon time. Often the temporal context of a poem is simply chronological, in the

sense that one statement or image must necessarily precede
another. At other times the temporal context is not strictly
chronological but rather, to use a desperate term, "conversational." The sequence of statements or images is not determined by chronology; instead it depends upon some sort
of association. When we read such poems we automatically
assume an empirical or common-sense time scheme. At any
rate we are not aware that they do violence to our ordinary
conception of the way things take place. None of the temporal implications of the poem, we find, differs very much
from the temporal implications of everyday conversation. All
such poems have, of course, a kind of time structure that
can be examined and related to the "rest of the poem," or
what I should like to call the "main" structure. But it is
not a conspicuous or dominant source of structure for the
poems. There are, on the other hand, poems which diverge
from the casual time scheme of conversation and which find
in their divergence a conspicuous, even a dominant, source
of strength and structure. Such poems seem first to appear
in the Baroque age. In fact, the use of time as a significant
structural device and, in more general terms, the poetic
awareness of "structural" time as contingent and manipulatable seem to be peculiar achievements of Baroque poets.

Even without subjecting any Baroque poem to structural
analysis, it is possible to show that some poets were explicitly aware of time as relative.[1] To pick a simple example,
let us consider a sonnet of Théophile de Viau (1590–1626):

> Je passe mon exil parmy de tristes lieux . . .
> Ou le Soleil, contrainct de plaire aux destinees,
> Pour estendre mes maux alonge ses journees,
> Et me faict plus durer le temps de la moitié . . .

Nothing, perhaps, can mitigate the flat exaggeration of the
poet's statement. And the climatic references can, perhaps,
be "explained" in terms of Théophile's exile in Holland. Yet

1. The meaning of "relative" is here intended to encompass the meaning
of the words "contingent," "manipulatable," and "subjective."

the directness of "Pour estendre mes maux alonge [not "*seems* to lengthen"] ses journées" distinguishes the assertion from the mere commonplace that time flies when we are happy and drags when we are sad. The hyperbole is reinforced as the poem continues and finally ends.

> Mais il [the sun] peut bien changer le cours de sa lumiere,
> Puis que le Roy perdant sa bonté coustumiere,
> A destourné pour moy le cours de sa pitié.[2]

Time and the sun's career are, in terms of the poem, actually made to depend upon the speaker's attitude. In the same spirit of exaggeration Honoré d'Urfé (1568–1625) writes of "moments paresseux." He carries out the conceit as far as possible:

> Moments, vous êtes jours, jours, vous êtes années,
> Qui de vos pas de plomb n'êtes jamais bornées,
> Que les siècles plus longs vous n'alliez égalant:
> Pénélope, de nuit, défaisait sa journée;
> Je crois que le Soleil va ses pas rappelant
> Pour prolonger le jour et ma peine obstinée.[3]

Both poems arrive at the same point, accusing the sun of malice in the interest of stressing their use of "subjective" time. One could go on citing instances from Baroque poetry (the most familiar would be Marvell's richly ironic manipulation of time in "To his Coy Mistress"), and it would still be possible to oppose them with earlier poems; but actually the novelty consists not in mere presence but in directness, in emphasis, and in frequency of occurrence.

Even on so simple a level time can to a certain extent be manipulated or conquered.[4] It can, to speak less metaphor-

2. Théophile de Viau, *Oeuvres poétiques*, ed. Jeanne Streicher, Geneva-Lille, 1951, première partie, p. 155.

3. "Sur une attente: sonnet de Céladon," in *Poésie du XVIIème siècle*, ed. Thierry Maulnier (Paris, 1945), p. 111.

4. Never, of course, could a poem actually conquer time, in the sense of becoming entirely independent of it; as, for similar reasons, never could a

ically, be put to more than casual uses. It is helpful to see that on a similar level and in a similar sense space can also be conquered. We may think of Donne in "The Sunne Rising" ("She'is all States, and all Princes, I") or in "The Canonization" (". . . Who did the whole worlds soule contract, and drove / Into the glasses of your eyes").[5] We may also think of Milton's use of space in *Paradise Lost* or the panoramic, almost hallucinatory shifts in space in "L'Allegro" and "Il Penseroso," or again, the juxtaposition of distant places as in "Lycidas" and later poems. And now and then we may come upon a complete reversal of ordinary spatial relationships. Take, for example, Gryphius' sonnet "Abend," in which we find the image: "Der port naht mehr und mehr sich zu der glieder kahn." [6] It is perhaps an extreme case; yet it is certainly not isolated, and it can easily be related to the examples of "subjective" time which have been quoted from French poets.

---

poem actually describe the mystical experience. It is more accurate to say that some poems go *about* trying to conquer time, or that so-called mystical poems *lead up to* the experience itself for which there can be no adequate objective correlative. See my essay, "The Rhetoric of Ineffability: Toward a Definition of Mystical Poetry," *Comparative Literature, 8,* 1956.

5. *The Poems of John Donne,* ed. H. J. C. Grierson (Oxford, 1912), *1,* 11, 15.

6. *Andreas Gryphius: lyrische Gedichte,* Bibliothek des litterarischen Vereins in Stuttgart, 171, ed. Hermann Palm, Tübingen, 1884. The reversal of spatial relationships is clear enough. But the expression "zu der glieder kahn" needs comment. The series of images which precede the quoted line are the approach of night, homecoming after work, loneliness, exhaustion of time. After the boat image a general lesson is drawn: they are all symbols of decline and death. "Glieder" may be taken to mean "body" by a sort of metonymy (see J. Grimm, *Deutsches Wörterbuch,* "Glied," IIE). The port, then, is death, and the "boat of limbs" the body. Compare also Marino's sonnet "Tranquillità notturna," in *Poesie varie,* ed. B. Croce (Bari, 1913), p. 99, which attempts poetically to transform the sea into the sky; and also "La nuit des nuits" of Du Bois Hus, in Thierry Maulnier and Dominique Aury, *Poètes précieux et baroques* (Anger, 1941), pp. 217–19, in which the sky in its reflection actually descends into the sea.

Pursuing the uses of time further, it is possible to see the same tendency to "conquer" time or to make it "relative" in much of the religious poetry of the Baroque age, particularly in such poets as Andreas Gryphius, Richard Crashaw, and Quirinus Kuhlmann, to mention no others. On the one hand, there is the constant preoccupation with the passage of time (hours, days, seasons), leading characteristically to contemplation of death and eternity. The tendency may even rush into utter paradox; night may become day and day night: "Je dunkler, je mehr lichter." [7] Particularly in German poetry of the age can one find frequent mention of the feebleness or illusory nature of time. Even the contrast between time and eternity may be denied, as in Angelus Silesius' epigram,

> Man sagt / die Zeit ist schnell; wer hat sie sehen fliegen?
> Sie bleibt ja unverrückt im Weltbegriffe liegen! [8]

In one way or another such statements depend upon the paradox of time seen under the aspect of eternity: time must have a stop and yet in terms of eternity it must have no end. The notion is thus distinguishable from the "topos" *tempus fugax,* which states a simple fact of experience and is not paradoxical; moreover, it cuts across the neat Thomistic categories of *tempus, aevum, aeternitas.* For an even more

7. Quirinus Kuhlmann, "Unio mystica" (taken from the *Kühlpsalter*), found in *Deutsche Barocklyrik,* ed. M. Wehrli (Basel, 1945), pp. 182–84. Compare Gryphius' sonnet in the same volume, pp. 124–25, "Über die Geburt Jesu," which ends, "Nacht, lichter als der Tag! Nacht, mehr denn lichte Nacht!" We should note in contrast that St. John of the Cross in his "Noche oscura" never tries to make the night any less night; it is rather the necessary condition in which the heart's "light" can "burn." Leonard Forster and A. A. Parker have shown in their article "Quirinus Kuhlmann and the Poetry of St. John of the Cross," *Bulletin of Hispanic Studies,* 35 (1958), 1–23, that Kuhlmann in his sixty-second "Kühlpsalm" translated from a Latin version of parts of several of St. John's poems.

8. *Cherubinischer Wandersmann,* Bk. V, no. 23, in G. Ellinger's edition, *Angelus Silesius: sämtliche poetische Werke* (Berlin, 1923), *1,* 174.

forthright version of the paradox we may go to Paul Fleming's "Gedanken über der Zeit":

> Ach dass doch jene Zeit, die ohne Zeit ist, käme
> und uns aus dieser Zeit in ihre Zeiten nähme,
> und aus uns selbsten uns, dass wir gleich könten sein,
> wie *der* itzt jener Zeit, die keine Zeit geht ein! [9]

And this probably is the last word, doctrinally if not poetically.

On the other hand, just as suggestive are the quantities of poems which are little else than long series of exclamations. By means of a constant imperative or present tense, the time in which the poem takes place is narrowed down to a point of instantaneousness. The whole procedure is a way of "conquering" time by reducing it to a minimum. We can see such a tendency, for example, in many of the poems in Friedrich von Spee's *Trutznachtigall* and in a number of Crashaw's poems, notably "The Flaming Heart." The imperative and repetitive style is even more marked in a poem like Kuhlmann's "Mystische Auffahrt." Take, as a sample, these lines:

> So stoss ich los in meines Gottes Schirm!
> Auf, Engel, Auf! Umschlüsset mich nun rings!
> Auf, Heilgen, Auf! Auf, jauchzt in dieser Uhr!
> Unendlich wird itz meines Herzens Mut!
> Unendlich wird mein Vorsatz fest in Gott! [10]

And the whole tendency seems to reach a kind of *ne plus ultra* in Gryphius' poem "Ewige Freude der Auserwählten," which strains to describe in instantaneous terms the actual experience of eternity; its dramatic context would properly be outside of time, and yet it attempts to work somehow *through* time toward eternity.

9. *Paul Flemings deutsche Gedichte*, Bibliothek des litterarischen Vereins in Stuttgart, 82, ed. J. M. Lappenberg (Stuttgart, 1865), p. 30.

10. In *Deutsche Barocklyrik*, ed. Wehrli, p. 30; again it is from the *Kühlpsalter*.

O! wo bin ich? O! was seh' ich? wach ich? träumt mir? wie
    wird mir?
Jesu! welcher vollust meer überschwemmt mein frölich hertz?
Welt, ade! glück zu, mein trost! gute nacht tod, angst und
    schmertz!
Ich find alles, alles lern ich, alles schau ich, herr! in dir.
Ich zuschmeltz in lauter wonne, Jesu! Jesu, meine zier!
O wie herrlich ists hier seyn! Erde deine freud ist schertz!
Jesu! ewig-gläntzend licht! (dunckel ist der sonnen kertz!)
Ach! wie funckeln deine schaaren! sternen flieht! hier
    schimmern wir.
Ihr, die ihr gluth und schwerdt verlacht, ob schon eur leib
    würd staub und aschen;
Ihr, die ihr euer reines kleid habt in dem blut des lamms
    gewaschen,
Rufft: hallelujah! Hallelujah! freud und leben!
Dir, dreymal einig ewigkeit! die alles in allen beherrschet
    und ziehret,
Sey unaussprechlich lob und ruhm und ehre, die dir nur
    alleine gebühret!
Dir, die sich ewig (hallelujah!) uns wil geben! [11]

As an attempt to set forth extratemporal events in so temporal a medium as poetry, Gryphius' sonnet can only fail.
But certainly as an attempt it is significant here in being
an extreme example of Baroque awareness of time; for it
tries to push time beyond its casual uses and even beyond
our empirical perception of it. We can hardly say, as Fritz
Strich does, that asyndeton is the basis of Baroque poetical
style; yet we have here a good example, among many, of
how the Baroque view of time as relative expresses itself
asyndetically. The important trait in all this is that time
seems no longer to be taken for granted.

    It would be possible to go on elaborating the evidence of
a new awareness of time. There are many instances of a more
or less obvious sort which could be quoted. In a full cata-

11. *Lyrische Gedichte*, ed. H. Palm, p. 157.

logue one could not omit, for example, Vaughan's "The Retreate," Marvell's "To his Coy Mistress," Henry King's "The Exequy," and Milton's *Paradise Lost*—to mention only English texts. At the expense of completeness, however, the question should be raised: What effect did the new awareness of time have upon the structure of poetry? By way of suggesting a partial answer, I propose to analyze from the point of view of time the structure of several major Baroque poems.

Though my chief concern is with the element of time, I shall always assume that it is part of the composite total structure of a poem. I shall attempt at least to indicate the other principal sources of structure and relate the element of time to them and thus to the total structure. Generally speaking it is impossible, when analyzing a particular element of structure, not to assume a great deal about a poem. What has been written, for instance, on theme and metaphor in the Baroque lyric I shall either bypass or take for granted in order to concentrate on neglected elements.

Turning our attention exclusively to time, we encounter an elementary distinction which maps important boundaries. In gross terms we have to do with the empirical perception of time as past, present, and future. In a given poem it may be either the time in which the narration or performance takes place or the time which is narrated or implied. The narrator of Góngora's "Polifemo," for instance, tells us that he composed the "Fábula" (the body of the poem) at dawn and implies that he is "performing" it at midmorning. Milton's "Nativity Ode," like "Lycidas," is narrated in an interval of time stretching from early morning to sunset. These are examples of what might be called *narrative* time. From it the poems derive a certain measure of structure. But much more important is the structure they derive from *narrated* time, which is implicit in the sequence of tenses and time references. It is this that I propose to discuss.[12]

12. See Günther Müller, "Erzählzeit und erzählte Zeit," *Festschrift Paul Kluckhohn und Hermann Schneider gewidmet* (Tübingen, 1948), pp. 195–212.

The structural implications of *narrative* time are obvious. A poem is always set in a matrix of narrative time, whether overt or covert. Only when overt does it claim our attention as a significant source of structure. In the lyric, overt narrative time is not very common and, where it occurs, not very fruitful; the genre, in contrast to the novel, does not seem to encourage its use. On the other hand, *narrated* time is widely used in overt ways. Particularly in many Baroque lyrics it is a major source of structure. We shall see that there are patterns of tenses, form-generating progressions, distinguished and fused planes of time. We shall see that they are related to the total structure of the poems we consider and that they are therefore closely bound to the "sense." A pattern of tenses, in other words, is a pattern of meaning.

In using the terms "tense" and "time reference" I am aware of their ambiguity and oblique relation. It is, of course, possible to distinguish rigorously between them. In combination with adverbs, for instance, verbs morphologically in the present tense may in context take on a future meaning. Future forms of the verb may actually signify habitual action. References made through other parts of speech may point to events or existences in past, present, or future. Moreover, the verb structures of different languages generate nuances that cannot be translated out of their linguistic context. For such reasons it seems justifiable to work with large and perhaps scientifically imprecise categories which are general enough to allow comparison of texts in several languages and which at the same time recognize actual meaning as well as grammatical form.

One final matter before proceeding to a conspectus of simple tense patterns. In writing narrative poetry, as in writing history, it has long been a convention to make use of what is commonly called the historical present. Indeed, in many languages it is quite natural when relating past events in conversation to revert to the present tense. Among influential poets particularly in Virgil and Ovid can one find numerous instances. The effect achieved by passages in the historical present is usually described as vividness. Where an isolated reversion to past or present occurs, it is often explained as metrically necessary. But certainly the reader is never confused as to when the action takes place. Although Góngora and Milton, especially, are subject to the influence of Latin practice, it seems to me that they are not merely taking advantage of the customary license. The very pattern of their use of time and their very subject matter express something quite new. Instead of invoking rhetorical license at random, they seem to have found a new means of structure. In general, the heightened awareness of time that one encounters in Baroque poetry would seem to permit a stressing of the distinctions rather than the similarities.

2. A Survey of Time Patterns

A reading of Milton's "Nativity Ode," with special regard for tense, brings to light characteristics of style which have not yet received proper notice. Even before reading the poem one naturally suspects from the full title, "On the Morning of Christ's Nativity," that it will be an anniversary piece, most likely cast in either of two separate time planes, that of the event or that of the speaker. The first two stanzas of the Introduction, in fact, open up both possibilities: "This is the Month, and this the happy morn" when Christ "Our great redemption from above did bring." And they suggest a third possibility: maintaining an equal status for both time planes. But in the two concluding stanzas of the Introduction the two time planes are merged, and in the "Hymn" itself the actual morning of Christ's birth and the morning of the speaker become one and the same. Doctrinally, of course, it is not a radical departure; that kind of paradox or correspondence is the staple of medieval religious art and arises directly out of liturgy. Yet poetically it is quite new; not an assumption of correspondence but an attempt by literary means at fusion. It is, then, no hazy merging for the sake

of convenience. The reader is not allowed to explain away
or overlook. For the speaker pinpoints the time when he
calls on his muse to witness the progress of the wise men as
they approach Bethlehem:

> See how from far upon the Eastern road
> The Star-led Wizards haste with odours sweet.[1]

And once the contemporaneity of the two time planes has
been established, the speaker is able to go still further and
verge into a hortatory future in terms of the new present.
Thus in the Introduction not only is the subject of the
"Hymn" itself stated but also its temporal orientation is
suggested; so that, although the "Hymn" may be considered
an artistic unity in itself, the Introduction serves to prepare
the reader and heighten his awareness. Despite the preparation, it is startling to discover right at the beginning of the
"Hymn" a seeming confusion of tenses:

> It *was* the Winter wild,
> While the Heav'n-born child,
>   All meanly wrapt in the rude manger *lies*.

A *while* clause might conceivably, within the bounds of
poetic license, take a present tense, though the main clause
be in the past. Yet in the next stanza "Nature's" actions at
the birth of Christ are described in the present tense. And
in the third stanza God allays Nature's fears in the past
tense. Peace, whom God *sent* down, "*came* softly sliding,"
and, "waving wide her myrtle wand, she," curiously enough,
"*strikes* a universal Peace through Sea and Land."

Clearly the consequences of such "confusion" have to be
faced. Is it shoddy technique or mere eccentricity? Or does
it have deeper meaning? Later we shall return to the "Nativity Ode," but first, considering in a general way the possibilities of time as a means of structure, let us inspect ex-

1. The text is from M. Y. Hughes, *Paradise Regained, the Minor Poems,
and Samson Agonistes* (New York, 1937), pp. 150–65. See below, pp. 171–79.

amples of the simpler uses of time in the Baroque lyric. Since the problem concerns the criticism of poetry in any age or in any language, it should first be dealt with in universal terms; once formulated, it then can possibly serve us as a measure of poetic achievement, a measure which, along with others, should help to define in the Baroque lyric those attributes historically dividing it from the Renaissance and medieval lyric.

But how is it that time can be used structurally and nonstructurally? Surely the tenses of every poem are a part of its structure. Indeed all discourse must occur in some sort of temporal context. Ordinary conversation, for instance, usually assumes a center in the present tense, from which it diverges sporadically and irregularly into past or future. Many poems are written in such a "conversational" time context; and from it they derive a certain unity, though usually to be successful they must depend more heavily on other means. An illustration of the "conversational" use of time might be taken almost at random from Petrarch.

> Io avrò sempre in odio la fenestra
> onde Amor m' aventò giá mille strali,
> perch' al quanti di lor non fûr mortali;
> Ch' è bel morir, mentre la vita è destra.
>
> Ma 'l sovrastar ne la pregion terrestra
> cagion m' è, lasso, d' infiniti mali;
> e piú mi duol che fíen meco immortali,
> poi che l' alma dal cor non si scapestra.
>
> Misera, che devrebbe esser accorta,
> per lunga esperienzia omai, che 'l tempo
> non è chi 'n dietro volga o chi l'affreni.
>
> Piú volte l' ho con ta' parole scorta:
> 'Vattene, trista; ché non va per tempo
> chi dopo lassa i suoi dí piú sereni.' [2]

2. The text is from *Le Rime sparse e i trionfi,* ed. E. Chiòrboli (Bari, 1930), p 76. A few unimportant changes in punctuation have been made.

All the tenses are represented, with the exception of the past indefinite; but they seem to form no pattern of their own. The time context, as the tone, is that of casual conversation. In fact, the future tense at the beginning ("I shall always hate the window") and the perfect tense toward the end ("Several times I have sent her off with such words") lack any sort of emphasis: their stylistic importance is small. It is rather the tone, the dramatic situation, and the completeness of thought which give the poem coherence. If, to take a fairly clear example, we look at Góngora's sonnet "De la Brevedad Engañosa de la Vida," we see time more obviously at work unifying the poem.

> Menos solicitó veloz saeta
>   destinada señal, que mordió aguda;
>   agonal carro por la arena muda
> no coronó con más silencio meta,
>   que presurosa corre, que secreta,
>   a su fin nuestra edad. A quien lo duda,
>   fiera que sea de razón desnuda,
>   cada Sol repetido es un cometa.
> ¿Confiésalo Cartago, y tú lo ignoras?
>   Peligro corres, Licio, si porfías
>   en seguir sombras y abrazar engaños.
> Mal te perdonarán a ti las horas;
>   las horas que limando están los días,
>   los días que royendo están los años.[3]

The movement of thought in the poem consists in the speaker's reaching into the past for examples to extend to Licio in the present as a warning against a possible future. At the same time the verbs progress from past to present to future, underscoring the argument of the poem. As it happens, the

3. In Góngora's *Obras completas*, ed. J. and I. Millé y Giménez (Madrid, 1943), p. 449. In this edition the sonnet is dated 1623. At first glance one naturally suspects direct borrowing from Horace; but that is not the case (cf. *Odes* 1.22).

verbs in the first quatrain are in the past definite, though they could easily have been in the present. That they are in the past definite we must accept as added strength for the time scheme. The dependent clause "que presurosa corre . . ." then brings about a shift to the present and makes a transition to the second quatrain, in which the moral lesson is stated in the present. At the beginning of the sestet the movement of the poem up to that point is emphasized in a present reference to a past event ("¿Confiésalo Cartago?"). Thereupon a warning in the present ("Peligro corres, Licio, si porfías") points to the future, which is finally established in "Mal te perdonarán a ti las horas." Góngora's sonnet, in contrast to Petrarch's, moves according to a discernible time pattern. We are therefore able to say at once that a comparison of the two poems, without proving in itself anything historically, shows that some poems depend more than others upon time as a structural means.[4] And, allowing a distinction which is not logically exclusive but nevertheless significant, we may conveniently speak of time used structurally and nonstructurally.

Movement toward the future, either full or incomplete, is perhaps the commonest movement to be found in the Baroque lyric. It had been common also in previous ages (see especially Petrarch or Wyatt), but had rarely assumed a complex or gradual form: usually the poem would begin with a reference to the past and then proceed to an application to the present. In contrast we see in the sonnet of Góngora quoted earlier a larger degree of complexity and gradualness. We notice a straining to reach into the past, from which the poem derives "momentum" as it gradually works into the future. Other examples could be chosen from Góngora and Marino, to mention only them, but particularly rich in "progressive" movement are the poems of Henry

---

4. Examples of movement from past to present to future can be found in Petrarch (e.g. Sonnet CVII), but the contrast between tenses is no greater than in casual conversation.

Vaughan. "The Night," "And do they so," or "They have all gone into the world of light," might be considered as illustrations; there would be a number of others which in greater or lesser degree may be said to move from the past toward the future. For the sake of clarity we may look at one of Vaughan's simpler poems, "The Law, and the Gospel." Rhetorically the poem is a monologue addressed to God. The speaker begins remotely in terms of "they" (the Jews), then "we" (Christians), then "I" (the particular Christian, the speaker). With an effect of emphasizing the trend of thought, the verbs move from past to present to imperative and future. Yet there is hardly any abruptness. At the beginning of the second stanza the transition from past to present is made by means of a dependent clause:

> But now since we to Sion came,
> And through thy bloud thy glory see,
> With filial Confidence we touch ev'n thee.[5]

The next transition is longer, beginning in stanza 3 and continuing in stanza 4. It consists of a series of imperatives, beseeching God to perform or prevent future possibilities. At last the future is established, coinciding with the climax of the poem.

> So Shall thy mercies flow: for while I fear,
> I know, thou'lt bear,
> But should thy mild Injunction nothing move me,
> I would both think, and Judge I did not love thee.

Thus, the simple future having been fully asserted, the poem ends on a statement of future possibility.

Examples of retrogressive movement are not nearly so plentiful. We could not consider as such the sort of poem, common in the Renaissance, which begins as a quotation in the present tense and ends with a description of the occasion

5. The text is from *The Works of Henry Vaughan*, ed. L. C. Martin (Oxford, 1914), 2, 465–66.

in the past; as, for example, "Thus spake Philistus, on his hooke relying: / And sweetly fell a dying." [6] For it is clearly mere perfunctory use of narrative time. In order to find many instances of retrogressive movement, structurally important, we would most likely have to go as far as the Romantic period.[7] There are, however, interesting examples in the Baroque. A sonnet of Lope de Vega shows retrogressive movement from the present to the past.

> Cuando el mejor planeta en el diluvio
> templa de Etna y volcán la ardiente fragua,
> y el mar, pasado el límite, desagua,
> encarcelando al sol dorado y rubio;
>   cuando cuelgan del Cáucaso y Vesubio
> mil cuerpos entre verdes ovas y agua;
> cuando balas de nieve y rayos fragua,
> y el Ganges se juntó con el Danubio;
>   cuando el tiempo perdió su mismo estilo,
> y el infierno pensó tener sosiego,
> y excedió sus pirámides el Nilo;
>   Cuando el mundo quedó turbado y ciego,
> ¿dónde estabas, Amor? ¿Cuál fué tu asilo,
> que en tantas aguas se escapó tu fuego? [8]

The poem begins in the present tense with easily acceptable exaggerations; but when the reader is called upon to accept the statement that "a thousand bodies hang from the Caucasus and Vesuvius in the midst of green seaweed and water," he may begin to rebel. Yet the speaker does not temporize. Instead he shifts into the past, thus stressing the historicity of the events described. And the reader comes to realize that

6. The quotation is from "Philistus farewell to false Clorinda" ("Out of M. Morleyes Madrigalls") in *Englands Helicon*, ed. H. Macdonald (Harvard, 1950), p. 139.

7. See for example Wordsworth's "London, 1802" and "To Milton."

8. From the *Rimas* of 1602. The text is in Lope's *Obras escogidas*, ed. F. C. Sáinz de Robles (Madrid, 1946), 2, 70–71.

it is not only any flood, exaggerated for effect, but also the great Deluge. At the resolution of the poem in the question "Where were you, Love?" the reader's confusion, chiefly a result of the shift in tense, serves to hold in balance past and present, general and particular. Love *keeps* its fire burning even in floods which affect volcanos; and it *kept* its fire burning even in the primeval Deluge. The particular "events" described both in past and present contribute to the generalization of Love's nature, its power and its ability to survive.

An interesting variation on progressive and retrogressive movement is Vaughan's poem "The Retreate." It begins with an elaborate description of a past state, the speaker's "Angell-infancy." Each of the dependent clauses that follow the main clause of the first two lines described in the past tense the state of innocence in terms of the "corruption" of the more recent past. It all leads to the establishment of the present in the lines,

> O how I long to travell back
> And tread again that ancient track! [9]

And the present, although no actual future verb is used, strains into the future, in order, so to speak, to achieve the past again. The speaker looks forward to the future as regression:

> That I might once more reach that plaine,
> Where first I left my glorious train . . .
> Some men a forward motion love,
> But I by backward steps would move,
> And when this dust falls to the urn
> In that state I came return.

Thus the end of the poem naturally points back to the beginning. In several ways the poem manages to conquer time by, in the Latin sense, circumventing it.

9. *Works,* ed. L. C. Martin, 2, 419–20.

One could go on cataloguing tense patterns. Alternating and symmetrical types could be discussed in great detail. It seems sufficient to have indicated first the existence and then the range of tense patterns to be found in the Baroque lyric. So rapid a survey, however, cannot but be incomplete, for each type has many variations. Hybrid types also exist, as well as original departures. It is the main purpose of this deductive catalogue merely to prepare the way for an intensive discussion of three "original departures"—that is, three poems which have a time structure not accurately reducible to any simple category.

3. Milton's "Nativity Ode"

At the beginning of the last section I pointed out the seeming confusion of tenses to be found in Milton's "Nativity Ode"; [1] and in doing so I tried to suggest the direction one might take in accounting for it. The other alternatives could perhaps find advocates. Is it not merely eccentric or careless detail which the reader is expected to overlook? Is it not something extraneous to the "sense" of the poem? An advocate of the first of these alternatives might hold that the verb *lies*, which comes as a surprise after *was*, is necessarily in the present tense because it has to rime with *sympathize*. It is a minor blemish, he would say, in comparison with the great virtues of the poem: does the poet not tell the reader that he composed it hastily? Yet the explanation hardly covers the change of tense in the third stanza, where it is

1. The text is in *Paradise Regained, the Minor Poems, and Samson Agonistes*, ed. M. Y. Hughes (New York, 1937), pp. 150–65. The *Ode* can be dated December 1629; for Milton himself, when he printed it in the 1645 edition of his poems, dated it 1629, and at the end of Elegy VI he tells us it was begun "sub auroram" on Christmas day. See J. H. Hanford, *A Milton Handbook*, 4th ed. (New York, 1946), p. 141.

said that God *sent* down Peace who *came* and *strikes* a universal concord. An advocate of the second alternative would have to take the same position in a more extreme form. He would not be bothered with explaining away inconsistencies but would say instead that the tense was a mere accident and had nothing to do with the meaning of the poem. He might deny the relevance of even the simplest contrast between tenses, not to mention the importance of certain other details. There remains, then, the problem of accounting for the confusion of tenses and drawing what lessons we can.

I have already tried to show how in the Introduction of the "Nativity Ode" the two time planes, deriving from the anniversary nature of the poem, become, in terms of the poem, contemporaneous. Their identification is established so strongly that in the last five lines of stanza 4 the tense can move without difficulty into what may be called a "hortatory future." The Introduction then not only states the occasion of the "Hymn" but prepares the reader for what is going to happen insofar as tense and structure are concerned. Therefore he is not startled to read:

> It *was* the Winter wild,
> While the Heav'n-born child,
>   All meanly wrapt in the rude manger *lies.*

Momentarily the next stanza may lead him to think that the present tense is "merely" an historical present:

> Only with speeches fair
> She *woos* the gentle Air . . .

But in stanza 3 the "confusion" appears again, inescapable. God's action at the birth of Christ is described in the past, but is carried out in the present ("She *strikes* a universal Peace through Sea and Land"). And once more the identification of the two time planes is reinforced; mostly by the switch in tense, but also partly by the rather loose sentence which contains a series of intervening phrases (lines 4 to 7) whose function is to make the switch as gradual and as natural as possible. In stanza 4 the details of the "universal Peace" are worked out in the past tense. But as the elaboration continues in stanza 5, the tense shifts again into the present. And again the change is brought about gradually, this time by means of a present participial clause and a relative clause in the present perfect tense. In fact, the reader is almost imperceptibly swung into the present: such is the effect of the "Whispering . . ." clause and the coupling of "now" with the present reference of "hath quite forgot to rave."

> The Winds, with wonder *whist,*
> Smoothly the waters *kiss't,*
> 　Whispering new joys to the mild Ocean,
> Who now *hath* quite *forgot* to rave,
> While Birds of Calm *sit* brooding on the charmed wave.

For a time, what we might call the present aspect of the temporal orientation (in the process of being established) continues. Stanza 6 begins in the present; then the pendulum swings back the other way, and it ends in the past. There is even a negative future or modal reference made in terms of the present. The stars *"stand* fixt . . . And *will not take* their flight" despite the dawn "Or Lucifer that often *warn'd* them thence." With the ambiguous "warn'd," which could stand for either a present perfect or a pluperfect ("has" or "had warned") and thus refer either to the preceding present or to the subsequent past tense, the stanza moves into the resolution of the thought, which takes place in the past tense: rather than scatter, the stars remained and *"did glow"* until God *"bespake,* and *bid* them go." [2]

2. "Bespake" means simply "spoke" (see *NED,* "Bespeak," 1, 2, where the passage is cited). And "Bid" is a past tense of the verb, instead of "bade." Milton uses the same form further along in the poem (line 124) and also in *Paradise Lost* (VIII, line 519). See Hughes' edition, p. 155; and *NED,* "Bid," paragraph B of variant forms.

In the next several stanzas the past tense is dominant. But it is not allowed to prevail and thus unbalance the "biplanar" orientation; for we do not wholly lose sight of the present, and soon the present comes to dominate the past. Stanzas 7 and 8 are consistently in the past: the sun *"withheld* his wonted speed" and the shepherds *"Sat* simply chatting in a rustic row." We are reminded in stanza 9 of the present time plane, as the air "still *prolongs* each heav'nly close" of the angelic music. And in stanza 11 the present becomes more assertive, almost freeing itself of the past. Stanza 12 refers to Creation, which of course antedates both planes of time; it thereby strengthens the dynamic identification of the two; and besides, it cushions the swing of the pendulum back to the present. But the movement of the tenses becomes more complicated. It is not a simple present into which we enter; it is rather an imperative, which by its nature directs us toward the future. And indeed the future is asserted in stanza 14 and remains in force through stanza 17. Thus in the space of a few lines the time scope of the poem is stretched to its farthest limits: the time of Creation and the hypothetical time of the union of heaven and earth. So great an expansion can take place without disturbing the two chief time planes of the poem and their identification because up to that point the two tenses, past and present, had alternated in so easy and intertwined a fashion that they thus established their paradoxical contemporaneity. And not only does the expansion not rend the time structure of the poem; it serves, in at least two ways, to strengthen it. First of all, the two references, to the "extreme" past and to an "extreme" hypothetical future, encircle the dynamic identification by bounding it. Secondly, there is almost a literal "encirclement"; for, we are told, if the celestial music continues for long, "Time *will run* back, and fetch the age of gold" (stanza 14). All the while we have the reference to Creation (stanza 12) in mind and think of the pristine innocence of the world, including man, which was in direct communion with heaven. Finally in stanza 15 the circularity of time is hypothetically fulfilled, when we are told,

> Yea, Truth and Justice then
> *Will* down *return* to men.

It is in this passage, after the biplanar identification has been thoroughly tested by the time references to extreme past and extreme future, that the climax of the poem occurs. But proof of this, relating time to sense, must wait until we have viewed the whole poem.

As we continue in our reading, we find that the hypothetical future into which the poem leapt was indeed "extreme." It is "retracted" at the admonishment of Fate:

> But wisest Fate says no,
> This must not yet be so,
>   The Babe lies yet in smiling Infancy,
> That on the bitter cross
> Must redeem our loss.
>   So both himself and us to glorify:
> Yet first to those ychain'd in sleep,
> The wakeful trump of doom must thunder through the
>   deep . . .

We are brought "down to earth" again in being reminded that the Christ child *is* still a child, and *will* grow up and suffer death on the cross. It is at this point that the tense, seen under the general aspect of the poem, begins to consolidate: as the poem continues, we shall see how the new present tense, standing for what was before an alternation between past and present, strengthens itself, until the poem ends serenely in a vivid momentaneous present. We come face to face in this stanza (16) with the central paradox of the poem, already implied in the biplanar identification of past and present: the Christ child was and is an infant, yet Christ must ascend the cross and die, as paradoxically He has done already. It is certainly a pardox familiar to Christians. Sinners are said to

crucify Christ; and Mass itself is a daily re-enactment of the
Last Supper or the Passion. Yet there is a difference: in Christian doctrine the paradox is only implicit; whereas in the
poem it is emphatic and poetically achieved through the
meaningful alternation of tenses and time references, in
such a way that, without disturbing the structure of the
poem, it may be directly faced. The way it is faced somewhat
mitigates its boldness. The Christ Child "lies" in the manger,
"That on the bitter cross / Must redeem our loss." There is
only a weak modal reference to the future, and that in terms
of a relative clause. In contrast, the main movement of the
sentence goes on to a far more distant future, referring to
the Day of Judgment. The two "extremes" we observed in
stanzas 12 to 15, Creation and the reconciliation of heaven
and earth are modified in stanzas 16 and 17: in the direction
of the past the reference goes back to Moses receiving the
Ten Commandments; and in the direction of the future the
reference goes forward to Judgment Day, "When . . . / The
dreadful Judge in middle Air shall spread his throne." With
stanza 18 we move, by way of a present tense with future
meaning ("And then at last our bliss / Full and perfect is"),
into the "new" present ("But now begins . . ."). It is a present tense which remains largely undisturbed throughout the
rest of the poem; a present tense which has resulted from the
fusion of the old past and present of the earlier stanzas.

Before the poem ends, there is a rather long passage
(stanzas 18 to 26) which describes the rout of the pagan
gods. We must ask ourselves: What is its function in terms of
the poem? and, more especially, What effect does it have
upon the time structure? Its relevance to the occasion of the
poem is quite clear, for it serves to illustrate some of the consequences of Christ's birth. In "dramatic" terms, the flight
of the pagan gods continues and contrasts with the action of
the coming of the angels: the movement of glorious arrival
finds its antithetical correspondence in the movement of
ignominious flight. The angels arrive in stanza 9 and the

effects of their song are described up to the end of stanza 15.
The tense moves from the "old" biplanar identification into
the hypothetical future. In contrast, after a stanza on the
Devil (18), the pagan gods begin to flee in stanza 19 and their
flight continues to be described until a transition is effected
in stanza 25. Insofar as tense is concerned, there is not the
same breadth of movement as in the passage on the angels; it
would be quite inappropriate, since the tense is in the
process of consolidating itself in the "new" present. As a
matter of fact, the passage on the pagan gods serves precisely
that purpose. It is all in the present (except for an incidental
present perfect in stanza 23 which in effect only strengthens
the prevailing present); and not only that, it is enhanced by
present participles and a gerund:

> Apollo from his shrine
> *Can* no more *divine,*
>   With hollow shriek the steep of Delphos *leaving.*
> The *parting* Genius *is* with *sighing sent.*

Moreover, the simple present verbs have a continuous force
to them: "inspires" (19), "mourn" (20), "moan" (21), "seems
to sweat" (21), "forgoes" (21), "shrinks" (22). Moloch having
just fled, his worshipers try to reinvoke him:

> In vain with Cymbals' ring
> They call the grisly king,
>   In dismal dance about the furnace blue.

Their action is one of continuous movement. And again in
vain, as if repeatedly in vain, the votaries of Osiris ("sable-
stoled Sorcerers") "bear his worship Ark" (24). Not only "is"
Osiris no longer "seen" (24), but all the pagan gods no
"Longer dare abide" (25); for

> Our Babe, to show his Godhead true,
> *Can* in his swaddling bands *control* the damned crew.

Using the modal auxiliary "can" strengthens the impression of progressive action.[3] The whole process is rounded out in the next stanza (26), where the setting of the sun is described in gradual terms. The tenses, however, are properly in a simple present form, for the poem is to end with an impression of narrowing down to a more precise momentaneous present. To that purpose, the last stanza (27) begins with an imperative ("But see!") addressed to the reader, which has, unlike many other uses of the imperative, a purely present, instantaneous connotation. The tense even goes into the present perfect in order to emphasize the momentaneous present by referring to an action in the immediate past:

> . . . the Virgin blest,
> *Hath laid* her Babe to rest,
>   Time is our tedious Song should here have ending;
> Heav'n's youngest teemed Star
> *Hath fixt* her polisht Car,
>   Her sleeping Lord with Handmaid Lamp attending . . .

So the poem ends, in as precise a present as possible:

> And all about the Courtly Stable,
> Bright-harness'd Angels *sit* in order serviceable.

The past tense has been left far behind. It is not that the poem emerges finally into an historical present: in terms of the structure of the poem and in terms of the central paradox, as we have seen, such a view would be too simple. The tense has been "achieved." The birth of Christ and every Christmas are essentially the same.

It may be useful to restate the tense structure of the "Nativity Ode" in more schematic terms. Though we may abandon any consideration of the means whereby the transitions articulate, we should gain at least a more concise and perhaps a clearer view of the way the poem from this perspective works. In the first part of the poem, as far as stanza 7, there

3. "Can" is also used twice in the preceding stanza (24) to the same end.

is a quite rapid alternation of tenses. The reader's time sense
is meaningfully confused. When the angelic hosts are about
to appear, and at their appearance, the alternation becomes
considerably less rapid. By way of the slower alternation we
reach the center of the poem (stanzas 12 to 17), where something new occurs. The exuberant joy caused by the celestial
music finds correspondence in the widening of the time
range. By now the two chief time planes, that of the speaker's
real time and that of the real birthday of Christ, are well
enough identified, so that the widening of the time range
does not affect their status. As we continue, we find that the
time range is revised in stanzas 16 and 17; the two extremes
are brought closer together. The whole process emphasizes
the identification of the two original time planes. In fact,
they are so closely identified that the tenses no longer alternate; a present tense carries the burden of both. In the
succeeding passage on the flight of the pagan gods, the
resonances of the "new" present tense find correspondence
in the pervasively progressive use of it. As the poem ends,
with the focus of interest narrowing again upon the Christ
Child, the extraordinarily progressive movement is braked
(beginning with the next to the last stanza) in a most interesting fashion. And at the very end the reader is gently eased
into a momentaneous present. In the barest terms we can
state the structure of the "Hymn" this way:

I Beginning (setting and Christ Child)	rapid alternation
II Angels	slower alternation
III Center	widening time range, strengthening identification
IV Devils	progressive present
V End (return to setting and Christ Child)	momentaneous present

Thus we see how much the time structure depends upon tense, and how closely tense is coordinated with meaning. All the main elements of the poem work toward the same end, achieving the almost ecstatic joy and, by transforming it, the final serenity.

If we push the consideration of time in the "Nativity Ode" a step farther, we can connect it with Christian eschatology. Surely no orthodox Christian view of time in the Baroque age would have doubted its reality. Time would naturally have a past, present, and future. Events in the past, such as the birth of Christ, would be considered, strictly speaking, *einmalig*. Yet time was thought of as bounded at either end.[4] Time began with the creation of the world, several thousand years before;[5] and it was expected to end in the not too distant future. Witness Sir Thomas Browne: "But in this latter Scene of time, we cannot expect such Mummies unto our memories, when ambition may fear the Prophecy of Elias [margin: 'that the world may last but six thousand years'], and Charles the fift can never hope to live within two Methusela's of Hector."[6] Whether or not the world itself was in decay would not matter: orthodoxy taught, however cau-

4. It is interesting to compare what Marjorie Hope Nicolson has to say about time bounded at either end, in connection with Donne's *Anniversaries;* see *The Breaking of the Circle* (Evanston, 1950), especially pp. 89–92.

5. See, by way of testimony, John Locke's *Essay Concerning Human Understanding*, ed. A. C. Fraser (Oxford, 1894), *1*, 254–55: "And if the common reckoning of 5639 years from Creation to 1689 should be true (as it may be as well as any other assigned), it hinders not at all my imagining what others mean, when they make the world one thousand years older, since every one may with the same facility imagine (I do not say believe) the world to be 50,000 years old, as 5639; and may as well conceive the duration of 50,000 years as 5639." Though Locke is obviously avoiding any quarrel with the view that the world was 5639 years old in 1689, and though his main concern is with "duration" rather than time, he seems to be stating the received, the theologically acceptable date of Creation. The important thing is that he, however indirectly, presents the common view and indicates, by his caution, its orthodoxy.

6. *Hydriotaphia*, in his *Works*, ed. G. Keynes (London, 1929), *4*, 45.

tiously, that the millennium was approaching. With the boundaries thus firmly set, it was possible to see time, under the aspect of eternity, as static and all moments as equally present. Time, therefore, could be considered contingent and to some extent manipulatable within the closed Christian system. We need not think that time was in any way held to be unreal. It is possible to go further and say that the Christian conception of time implied circularity. The second coming of Christ was expected at the future end of time; it would be the re-establishment of Paradise much as it had existed in the beginning.[7] Milton in *Paradise Lost,* for example, calls upon his "Heav'nly Muse" to sing of the whole expanse of human history from "loss of Eden" to the time when "one greater Man / Restore us, and regain the blissful Seat." These implications of Christian doctrine are set forth in the "Nativity Ode," as we have seen, quite explicitly in the eschatological vision of stanzas 12 and following. Indeed, the Christian ideas of the circularity of time and the simultaneity of all moments under the aspect of eternity underlie the innermost structure of the poem. For all these reasons we must be wary of easy formulations of Baroque originality. Doctrinally it hardly consisted in any radical departure from tradition; it rather develops certain implications already latent in orthodoxy and tends to emphasize them. It is the emphatic and overt poetic use to which time is put that may be characterized as Baroque.

Milton's "Ode" is by no means an isolated example of the new emphasis and its embodiment in poetry. We shall find similar confusion of tenses in, for example, Góngora's "Polifemo" (1613), the next poem to be considered, and it is present there in an even more extreme form. Although Góngora is undoubtedly influenced by the Christian conception of time, his subject and his treatment of it are entirely

7. Christian teaching, of course, has obvious analogues in some forms of pagan primitivism. See A. O. Lovejoy and G. Boas, *A Documentary History of Primitivism and Related Ideas* (Baltimore, 1935), Vol. 1.

secular. The "Polifemo" should, therefore, provide a broader base for generalization. In a fairly distinct poetic tradition, though, of course, in the same cultural tradition, Góngora affords a striking parallel to Milton's practice. The similarity goes farther than mere coincidence, and at least suggests the possibility of demonstrating a common Baroque tendency.

4. Góngora's "Polifemo"

It is sometimes hard to decide how to classify a poem, whether as lyric or as narrative. We might say that Marlowe's "Hero and Leander" is a narrative poem, and Crashaw's "Musicks Duell" a lyric. Yet both of them have in common the problems of presenting a more or less unified action and of varying skillfully the mode of presentation. Marlowe, following the usual medieval and Renaissance practice, as well as common sense, casts his narrative in the past tense. The present he reserves for its conversational uses: as, for instance, the speaker's comments ("but my rude pen / Can hardly blazon foorth the loues of men"), general reflections (" 'Tis wisedome to giue much, a gift preuailes, / When deepe perswading Oratorie failes"), and direct discourse.[1] There is practically no use of the historical present.[2] All the while, despite

1. The quotations are lines 69–70 of the First Sestiad and lines 226–27 of the Second, as printed in the *Works of Christopher Marlowe*, ed. C. F. Tucker Brooke, Oxford, 1910. The poem could not have been written later than 1593; and it probably was not written much, if at all, before.

2. Lines 313–14 of the First Sestiad do contain a relative clause in the present tense.

such conventional uses of the present tense, the reader is
never allowed to lose his awareness of the fact that all the
events described are, with respect to the speaker, very much
in the past. Crashaw also faces the same problems in "Musicks Duell." [3] But he restricts himself to only one of the
devices which Marlowe might have used and remains within
the bounds of traditional "decorum," that is, the historical
present. We are introduced to the poem and the "plot" in a
short passage cast in the past tense. And when the poem
slides into the present, we recognize the "historical" use of
it; though we may notice how untraditionally the shift is
made (lines 15–17):

> The man perceiv'd his Rivall, and her Art,
> Dispos'd to give the light-foot Lady sport
> Awakes his Lute . . .

I say "slide" because the looseness of the sentence itself (the
uncertain syntactical relation of the clause beginning with
"dispos'd") sets the reader adrift. The poem then continues
in the historical present, except for two brief reversions to
the past (lines 27–29 and 105), which seem to have little
structural importance. They do serve to remind us for a
while that the poem is cast in the historical present. But in
the last third of the poem (lines 106–68) the reader loses sight
of the historical present and is led into what seems, with
respect to the speaker, an actual present tense. In fact, the
reader is almost called upon to witness the death of the nightingale:

> Shee failes, and failing grieves, and grieving dyes,
> Shee dyes; and leaves her life the Victors prize,
> Falling upon his Lute; o fit to have
> (That liv'd so sweetly) dead, so sweet a Grave! [4]

3. The text is in the *Poems, English, Latin and Greek, of Richard Crashaw*,
ed. L. C. Martin (Oxford, 1927), pp. 149–53.

4. There is almost no authority for Crashaw's elaborate gradualness in the
poem he was paraphrasing. For these final lines, the original, a very popular

Here is a good example of how such a conventional narrative device as the use of the historical present is transformed and becomes a means of structure, in the sense in which we have been using the word. The poem begins, as we saw, traditionally enough; but as we follow it out, we see that there is an unexpected structuring in the progression from past to historical present to actual present.[5] And the structuring is all the more effective in that it is gradual: the transition from past to historical present has already been mentioned; we are kept aware that the present tense is historical by the two reversions to the past; and the transition from historical to actual present is begun in the direct discourse of lines 106–10 and completed in the final lines, 165–68.

Reading Marlowe's poem, we run no risk of losing our time sense. Despite occasional interruptions, the narrative proceeds unruffled on one time plane; and though the poem remains unfinished, there is no reason to suppose that it would not have continued just so. On the other hand, Crashaw's poem departs from the usual narrative technique and works out a structure in terms of a progression of tenses.

Any distinction between narrative and lyric poetry is hard to apply. It becomes even harder when we consider such a poem as Góngora's "Polifemo," which takes about 500 lines to recount the legend of Acis and Galatea.[6] Since he had set out, among other things, to tell a story, Góngora faced the problem of presenting a unified action. But rather than follow usual practice, as did Marlowe, and proceed along a more or less straight line, he departed from it in a most unusual way. The result is that the "Polifemo," though it de-

---

poem written by the Jesuit Famianus Strada (1572–1649), has "Deficit & vitam summo in certamine linquens / Victoris cadit in plectrum, par nacta sepulcrum." See the text which Martin quotes in his "Commentary," pp. 438–39.

5. "Actual" refers, as it does above, to the speaker's time.

6. In Ovid, the direct source, the legend is told in about 160 lines (*Metamorphoses* 13.738–897).

rives from the ordinary mythological narrative poetry of the Renaissance, must be classed as something in between narrative and lyric; closer to the latter, I would say, than to the former. In that it presents a unified and complex action, it is narrative; in that it slights the action and, along with other attributes, develops a structure of tenses, it is lyric. As the analysis proceeds, the "true nature" of the poem should become clear: the peculiar tense structure, the almost hallucinatory presentation of action, in short, the whole time orientation of the poem.[7]

At the beginning there are three stanzas dedicating the poem to the Conde de Niebla. Although they have no organic relevance to the poem itself, they have important functions, artistic as well as social. On learning that the poet's muse is Thalia, the reader is forewarned that the poem will partake more of comedy than tragedy. And the emphasis on the bucolic nature of the poem ("bucólica Talía," "la zampoña mía") gives the reader an inkling of how it will proceed. The reader is made aware of the poem as performance, particularly by the statements "Estas . . . rimas . . . escucha" and "en cuanto . . . escuchas . . . del músico jayán el fiero canto." Seen under the aspect of time, the Dedication shows an interesting form. It begins with an account in the past tense of the poet's source ("Estas que me dictó, rimas sonoras"); and moves on to the present, calling on the Count, in a series of imperatives, to leave his usual pursuits and listen to the performance of the poem. Finally, the Dedication slips into the future as the poet predicts, *musa volente,* the success of the poem. It is almost as if he were running through the gamut of tenses, as a preliminary fanfare before launching into the poem itself.

7. The text is from Luis de Góngora y Argote, *Obras completas,* ed. Juan and Isabel Millé y Giménez (Madrid, 1943), pp. 535–47. It is based upon Alfonso Reyes' edition (Madrid, 1923) and made to conform with R. Foulché-Delbosc's reading of the Chacón Manuscript (New York, 1921): see p. 1085 in Millé. The accepted date of composition of the *Polifemo,* as given by the Chacón Manuscript, is 1613. For the text, see below, pp. 180–213.

Rather unexpectedly, the poem proper begins in the present tense. Had it followed the common pattern, it would have begun like "Hero and Leander" in the past. Throughout the description in the first three stanzas of the coast of Sicily and the dwelling place of Polyphemus, the tense remains present. It is only in stanza 4 that it changes, quite suddenly, into the past indefinite. Polyphemus' size is described: in the past, perhaps in order to command belief more easily. Also, the shift into the past indefinite makes it possible for the speaker to stress habitual or continuous action (stanza 4):

> cíclope a quien el pino más valiente,
> bastón, le obedecía tan ligero,
> y al grave peso junco tan delgado,
> que un día era bastón y otro cayado.

In stanza 6 we encounter the same thing, this time contrasted with a preceding present tense:

> pellico es ya la que en los bosques era
> mortal horror, al que con paso lento
> los bueyes a su albergue reducía,
> pisando la dudosa luz de el día.

In between the two passages there is a whole stanza (5) in the present. And after stanza 6, which alternates between past definite, present, and past indefinite, there are two stanzas in the present (7 and 8). Thus the whole passage presenting Polyphemus continues in slow alternation between past and present (stanzas 4 to 9). Even in some of the passages in the present tense the past is asserted faintly in a dependent clause; see stanza 7, line 6, and stanza 8, line 6.[8] In contrast to the way in which Polyphemus is introduced, Galatea is described chiefly in the present. The first mention of her is in the present, and continues for two stanzas (10 and 11). Briefly, in the next two stanzas (12 and 13) the narrative dips into the past indefinite and then the past definite; but

---

8. Henceforth the form 7.6 and 8.6 will be used.

it remains predominantly present, and continues almost entirely undisturbed as far as stanza 20.[9] All the while, interest centers upon Galatea, the "fugitive nymph," who is being pursued by Glaucus, a god of the sea. In stanza 20 she finally discovers a haven and is lulled by nightingales. Then suddenly the poem moves back to the past as, in stanza 21, Acis makes his first appearance; the next stanza (22) describes him in the past indefinite (as Polyphemus had been described); and the stanza following (23) tells in the past definite his action in placing his gift of almonds, butter, and honey by the side of the sleeping Galatea. Acis' next action is told in the present, beginning a passage of six stanzas in which there is an easy oscillation between present and past (24 through 29). The sense of the passage oscillates too, for in it Galatea is awakened by the sound of Acis splashing water. She is about to flee when she is seized by a "lazy fear"; Cupid intervenes and shoots her with an arrow, and she falls in love with the donor of the gift. As she hesitated before to flee, now she hesitates to call out, because she does not know his name. Finally, she seeks him out and finds him pretending to be asleep.

Beginning with the second line of stanza 30, the alternation between present and past ceases, and we enter upon a new phase of the action, which is consistently set forth in the present tense. The passage describes Galatea suspended over the prone form of Acis, as she is feasting with her eyes upon his lineaments and as he is watchfully feigning sleep. He gradually shows his interest in her, and once she has raised him up they retire to a recess under a cliff, and the tense tactfully switches to the past, bringing the long passage in the present to a close. As they carry on their love-making the tense, beginning with stanza 38, changes to the present and remains there for two stanzas. Then, to reintroduce the lovesick Polyphemus, the tense reverts to the past: in stanza 40 he

9. Stanza 14 moves from a past subjunctive with present optative meaning to a weak future of probability and back to the present. This, together with two incidental, completely nonstructural references to the past in 17.7 and 18.2, constitutes the only divergence from the present tense.

takes up his position on a jutting rock and in stanza 41 he sounds his pipes, frightening Galatea. Stanza 42 continues to tell of Galatea's fear, but it has gone into the present, pointing up the immediacy of the situation. Thus the passage of slow alternation between past and present (from 36.5 through 42) ends, and we go into the third and longest of the three long passages in the present which are to be found in the poem. Except for four fleeting instances of other tenses,[10] there are seven whole stanzas (56 lines) in the present tense. It is perhaps only to be expected that the passage should be in the present, since it consists almost entirely of Polyphemus' address to Galatea, in which he invokes her with praise and sets forth his own merits.

But soon, in the midst of his speech, Polyphemus begins to search for examples of his might and hospitality. In stanza 50 his discourse goes into the past; in stanza 51 it returns to the present and then goes into the past again. Throughout the rest of the speech the same alternation continues: passages in the past of 8 to 12 lines alternate with shorter passages in the present. And when the speech ends, the oscillation between tenses goes on, more and more hectically, up to the end of the poem. How Polyphemus is interrupted by his goats, and how he accidentally discovers the whereabouts of the lovers, we find narrated in the past. Then the alarm and flight of the lovers appear in the present (stanza 57). But quickly the past returns when we are told of the hares they scattered in their haste. Immediately afterward, in stanza 58, there is a long present participial clause, then a short clause in the past definite, finally resolving in the present. The resolution occurs in the lines:

> y al garzón viendo, cuantas mover pudo
> celoso trueno, antiguas hayas mueve.

Polyphemus is the subject; it is he who "could move"—that is, shake the "ancient beechtrees." The very next phase of his action brings us to the past again (59):

10. See 42.4, 43.6–7, 43.1, 48.7.

> Con violencia desgajó, infinita,
> la mayor punta de la excelsa roca . . .

But we are jerked from the past definite back into the present as the passage continues:

> . . . que al joven, sobre quien la precipita,
> urna es mucha, pirámide no poca.

For a short while the present tense remains; at the end of stanza 59, however, the tense again suddenly reverts to the past. The sentence structure itself seems quite loose:

> concurren todas, y el peñasco duro,
> la sangre que exprimió, cristal fué puro.

The past continues to hold sway in the first half of the next and final stanza (60). Yet the second half begins with present participial clauses and reaches a direct present tense:

> Corriendo plata al fin sus blancos huesos,
> lamiendo flores y argentando arenas,
> a Doris llega . . .

This final appearance of the present tense is only very brief, for the poem closes with the next line and a half in the past:

> . . . que con llanto pío,
> yerno le saludó, le aclamó río.

Though his time sense has been meaningfully confused, the reader can thus take leave of the poem with a sense of pastness, as the last of his impressions.[11]

---

11. Obviously Góngora's tenses reflect Latin poetic license: Ovid especially makes constant use of the historical present. In Ovid's version of the story Galatea relates her adventures to Scylla in direct discourse. Her use of the present tense, then, is what one may accurately call "conversational." Góngora most certainly had his Latin model in mind; yet the great difference still remains that he, in contrast to Ovid, used mainly impartial narrative and not direct discourse and that he achieved in the end a structural pattern of tense.

All the same, the reader is left at the end of the "Polifemo" with no guarantee that the same action will not happen again or does not happen repeatedly. The effect is achieved partly through the alternation of tenses and partly through the mode of presenting action. We have observed the way in which alternation of tenses cuts the reader adrift from any common-sense orientation in time; the kind of orientation which traditional narrative poetry makes use of, even in its obvious use of the historical present. It is interesting to find that also the action is often telescoped in such a way that much seems almost to be taken for granted.[12] We are told, for instance, that Polyphemus is in love with Galatea (10); yet when she is presented, her attitude toward him is not made clear, though we must assume that she is trying to avoid him. The figure of Polyphemus, described at length in the first part of the poem and somewhat neglected in the middle (despite the vague way he is related to the action concerning Acis and Galatea), broods over the narrative even though there is no overt mention of the danger he represents and even when he himself does not appear for some time. It could be shown in greater detail how the manner of presenting action contributes to the effect of timelessness or, perhaps more accurately, of permanent suspension.

We are mainly concerned, however, with how the effect is achieved by the use of tense. Analyzing the poem from the point of view of time has uncovered a discernible structure which can now be stated in summary form. At the beginning, after an unusual but comfortable start in the present and an abrupt switch to the past, we became aware of a measured oscillation between the two tenses. Polyphemus was introduced in the past and a little later Galatea in the present. But starting at stanza 15 we encountered a fairly long passage of six stanzas entirely in the present. Here there seemed to be a preparation for the main action, ranging from vague fore-

12. Partially, at least, Góngora's allusiveness must be attributed to an assumption that the reader has close acquaintance with his source in Ovid.

bodings to Galatea's finally finding a resting place. Acis then appeared in the past tense (three stanzas); and after another oscillating passage, the narrative emerged, with the meeting of Acis and Galatea, again into a long passage of somewhat more than six stanzas in the present tense. Next came the lovers' dalliance in oscillating tenses. And we were led to the third and last long passage in the present, this time of eight stanzas, which concerned the coming of Polyphemus and the first part of his speech. As he became more and more shrill in his own self-praise, losing himself in detail, the tenses began to alternate again. As Polyphemus discovered the lovers and went into action, the oscillation became more and more rapid. The lovers "seek" the ocean and "scattered" the hares on their way. Polyphemus violently "tore loose" the peak of a cliff and "dashes" it over Acis. And finally, Acis, his crushed body having turned into liquid silver, "reaches" Doris (representing a river), who "greeted" him as a son-in-law and "acclaimed" him as a river.

It is interesting to note that the tense structure that reveals itself never conflicts with the movement of the poem in terms of plot; in fact, it gives it unexpected strength, as well as a new dimension. Moreover, this tense not only underscores the main turns in the action of the poem but also contributes an important movement of its own. There is a battle of tenses going on throughout the poem, a battle for supremacy between present and past. During the first two-thirds of the poem the present asserts itself more and more strongly. Then the past, which has fought only a sustaining action, begins to take over, as if the present had expended itself by overexertion. And the poem ends as the two tenses seem to be in equal struggle, with some advantage to the past which closes the poem. Partly the sense of struggle derives from the norm against which one reads the "Polifemo." Nothing of the sort goes on in, for example, Marlowe's "Hero and Leander." Nor are we aware of struggle in the use of tenses in Crashaw's "Musicks Duell." Góngora has gone beyond Crashaw in complexity. If we followed strictly the categories of tense structure that we have established, we should probably have to class the "Polifemo" as "alternating"; yet it is certainly a very special instance, and practically creates its own category. It is also possible, perhaps, to squeeze the plot into the usual scheme and say that it has a beginning, middle, and end. Yet it seems more important to emphasize the air of foreboding that gradually thickens around the figure of Polyphemus and the driving and inexorable fatality that increasingly impels the lovers: processes whose resolution takes place rapidly in the last few stanzas, as the present tense seems to lose its ascendency and fitfully subsides. In many ways, then, the poem gives us insight into the possibilities of structure in terms of tenses, or, somewhat more generally, time structure. Though the whole gamut touched in the Dedication was not employed, since the future tense does not enter significantly into the poem's structure, the elaborate and uncommon use of time fulfills the promise of virtuosity.

5. Milton's "Lycidas"

In "Lycidas" [1] there is also a demonstrable time structure; but it is not so obviously a patterning of tenses. Our time sense is not so openly confused as in the "Nativity Ode" or the "Polifemo." Yet even a perfunctory reading of "Lycidas" may leave in the mind a certain impression of confusion. Does it not come as something of a surprise to find that the last eight lines, contrary to the main tense of the poem, are in the past? Why does the poem say, in the midst of a passage in the present, "Phoebus repli'd?" And what relation to the whole structure does the change in tense in these lines have?

1. The text is from Milton's *Paradise Regained, the Minor Poems, and Samson Agonistes,* ed. Hughes, pp. 284–97. The date of composition, discernible in the Cambridge Manuscript, is November 1637. "Lycidas" was first published in 1638 as Milton's contribution to the volume *Obsequies to the Memory of Mr. Edward King,* and later reprinted with a few minor changes in Milton's collection of his own *Poems* (1645). See Hanford, *A Milton Handbook,* p. 166. Hughes' text is based on the edition of 1645 rather than that of 1638. Spelling is normalized, but capitals, italics, and contractions are retained. In order to avoid confusion with my italics, I have not followed the text in italicizing proper names. For the text, see below, pp. 214–19.

> But now my Oat proceeds,
> And listens to the Herald of the sea
> That came in Neptune's plea.

Such questions seem to depend upon the time structure of the poem. In contrast to the "Nativity Ode" and the "Polifemo," we note at once that the time structure of "Lycidas" is neither outwardly so striking nor inwardly so various. One does not encounter at a glance the almost bizarre alternation of tenses; nor does one discover, searching deeper, the near-violent conflict and resolution. From the start the poems assume different degrees of awareness. The "Nativity Ode" relies on the universal knowledge of Christ's birth and its attendant circumstances; the "Polifemo" relies upon a plot from Ovid; whereas "Lycidas" cannot necessarily presuppose a time perspective but must set out to construct one. In fact, it is just this process of discovering the time perspective which gives "Lycidas" its characteristic movement and structure.

At the beginning of the poem the reader is immediately made aware of a speaker discoursing in the first person and in the present tense. He disclaims his fitness to perform the ceremonies of mourning the dead; but then, he asks,

> Who would not sing for Lycidas? he knew
> Himself to sing, and build the lofty rhyme.

The tense has gone into the past, setting up a contrast between the present time of the performance and the past time when Lycidas was still alive. Next the speaker identifies his own fate with that of the dead Lycidas, first in a modal statement verging into the future ("So may some gentle Muse / With lucky words favour my destin'd Urn") and then in a long passage in the past tense ("For we were nurst upon the self-same hill"). In effect two time planes are thus firmly established: the speaker's present and the remote past of Lycidas' and the speaker's youth. In the next "section" (lines

37–49) the present tense is reasserted, as the loss of Lycidas is stated directly in terms of nature and the "shepherds." Changing to the present serves as preparation and contrast for the first direct reference to the actual event of Lycidas' death, which occurs in the lines addressed to the nymphs:

> Where were ye Nymphs when the remorseless deep
> Clos'd o'er the head of your lov'd Lycidas?

Because the time when Lycidas was drowned is less remotely in the past than the earlier references to him living, and because the two times are hitherto equally stressed, we are justified in considering the time of drowning as a separate time plane. Gradually the poem works out of the past ("Ay me, I fondly dream!"), despite the passing reference to Antiquity, and emerges into a general present. It is actually a return to the first time plane, that of the speaker "performing" his discourse. "Alas!" he exclaims,

> What boots it with uncessant care
> To tend the homely slighted Shepherd's trade,
> And strictly meditate the thankless Muse?

The whole passage continues thus, posing its ultimate question in the present tense. What, then, is the force of

> "But not the praise,"
> Phoebus *repli'd,* and *touch'd* my trembling ears? [2]

Why is it in the past? To begin with, the past tense informs the reader that the question stated in the present tense as a part of the performance of the poem, was in reality first asked in the less remote past, presumably just after the death of Lycidas. In a very telescoped way, therefore, we are again made aware of the contrast between the speaker's time and the time of Lycidas' death. It is a complex way of serving the exigencies of performance and structure at the same time. [3]

2. The quotation marks are mine.

3. John Crowe Ransom is worried by what he calls "an incredible interpolation"—the change to past tense and narrative discourse implied in the

In the next section of the poem, beginning with line 85, we encounter a continuation of the same effect.

> O Fountain Arethuse, and thou honour'd flood,
> Smooth-sliding Mincius, crown'd with vocal reeds,
> That strain I *heard* was of a higher mood:
> But now my Oat *proceeds*,
> And *listens* to the Herald of the Sea
> That *came* in Neptune's plea.
> He *ask'd* the Waves, and *ask'd* the Felon winds,
> What hard mishap hath doom'd this gentle swain?

"That strain," Phoebus' reply, is referred to consistently in the past. Then the impression of the poem as performance is continued in the present tense of "proceeds" and "listens." Moreover, those two verbs carry the weight of the transition from section to section, and provide a contrast with the new past tense of the following lines. Neptune's advocate is, of course, Triton; he, along with Camus and Peter, appears in a procession of mourners or apologists, who are all described in the past.[4] Their appearance defines another time plane, in the recent past with respect to the speaker's present; that is, in a past more recent either than that of Lycidas' "shepherd" days or that of his death. Though this passage is set forth in the past tense, we can see how closely that past tense approaches the present. Triton, the first of the three figures, is

---

lines (85–92) just quoted. But the passage is hardly an "interpolation" nor is it "incredible." It serves a complex function in terms of the time structure and also, as we shall see later, in terms of the rhetorical structure of the poem. See Ransom's essay on "Lycidas," "A Poem Nearly Anonymous," in *The World's Body* (New York, 1938), pp. 24–27.

4. The lines on the corrupt clergy (113–31) came from the mouth of Peter, and are reported in the form of direct discourse; they do not, therefore, constitute a new development in the tense structure, but merely a ramification of it. The fact that they are in the present tense emphasizes the aspect of the poem as performance and its dramaticality. A new interpretation of the unnamed "Pilot" as Christ at least points up the ambiguity of Milton's allusive phrase; see Ralph E. Hone, "'The Pilot of the *Galilean Lake*,'" *Studies in Philology, 56* (1959), 55–61.

hardly a mourner; his concern over the death of Lycidas is more remote than that of the others.[5] His function is to help narrow the blame for the drowning of Lycidas. Camus, next in the procession, is less remote, being more closely concerned that it was Lycidas and not, say, an Oxonian, who drowned, and also representing, as he does, a later stage in the series of repercussions from Lycidas' death. With Peter, the last of the three, direct concern over the actual death changes into a general lesson, a cause for universal mourning. His reported speech, cast in direct discourse and in the present tense, facilitates the transition to the next extended passage. It leads directly into:

> Return Alpheus, the dread voice is past,
> That shrunk thy streams; Return Sicilian Muse,
> And call the Vales, and bid them hither cast
> Their Bells and Flowrets of a thousand hues.

Thus the flower passage continues: entirely in the present. It is the first long passage which implies a time plane identical with that of the speaker. By means of it we emerge from the recent past directly into the speaker's present. In this way the reader's focus is refined to the extent of narrowing upon the plight of Lycidas at the mercy of the waves.

As we have seen, there has been a gradual progression from the remote past to the present; and with each stage the sharpness of grief for Lycidas' death has been intensified. The newest stage begins with the flower passage; but that hardly serves even "to interpose a little ease," for there can be no "Laureate Hearse." There is nothing to do but face, in terms of the present, the actual fate of Lycidas. The helpless uncer-

---

5. It is true that in the passage on Triton's testimony the tense momentarily breaks through into the present: "They knew not of his story / And sage Hippotades their answer *brings*, / That not a blast was from his dungeon stray'd." Again, the isolated use of the present does not disturb the tense structure; rather, it continues the impression of performance and points up how closely the new past approaches the speaker's present. It could be seen as a use of the historical present.

tainty of lines 152–64 ("Ay me! Whilst thee the shores, and sounding Seas / Wash far away . . .") emphasizes the instantaneousness of the moment and the utter hopelessness of mourning. Yet the general resolution of the time scheme and also the sense of the poem cannot be delayed any longer. The reader has been prepared by the merging of time planes; and he is further prepared when he reads,

> Weep no more, woeful Shepherds weep no more,

and goes on to the simile of the setting and rising sun. The completion of the simile contains the central paradox and pivot of the time scheme of the poem:

> So Lycidas, sunk low, but mounted high . . .

More will be said about the central paradox later. For the moment, concentrating on the time scheme, we may consider the phrase "sunk low" as referring to the past and to the old present before there was any intimation of an escape from hopeless mourning. On the other hand, "but mounted high" refers to the new present, a present continuing into the future. The whole richly elliptical phrase has the force of "Lycidas, who had sunk low, but is now mounted high . . ." And the continuing present carries the reader on through the rest of the passage. The risen Lycidas' life in heaven is quite naturally described in terms implying continuous iterative action:

> With Nectar pure his oozy Locks he *laves*,
> And *hears* the unexpressive nuptial Song,
> In the blest Kingdoms meek of joy and love.
> There *entertain* him all the Saints above,
> In solemn troops, and sweet Societies
> That *sing*, and *singing* in their glory *move*,
> And *wipe* the tears for ever from his eyes.

Even wiping away the tears *for ever* seems to imply duration, though the verb alone would refer merely to one action; indeed, standing as it does in a series of continuous present verbs, "wipe" itself takes on some of their character and thus greater suggestiveness. Having been reinforced by such means, the continuing present is further strengthened by a reassertion of the aspect of performance.

> Now Lycidas the Shepherds weep no more;
> Henceforth thou art the Genius of the shore,
> In thy large recompense, and shalt be good
> To all that wander in that perilous flood.

Finally, the whole ceremony of mourning has been performed; and, as if by way of reward, the cause for inconsolable grief has been dispelled. Even sorrow for Lycidas' absence from earth is mitigated by the announcement that he is the "Genius of the shore." His new function, which, in a sense, reconciles him with his fate, is spoken of in terms of the future. Thus, on a note of reconciliation, the main part of the poem ends, with the speaker's present victorious and, from that vantage point, with a gesture toward the future.

It may seem somewhat bewildering, then, that the final eight lines should go into the past. We must ask ourselves: What is their relation to the whole structure and, in particular, to the time scheme of the poem? In the barest terms, the whole poem follows a form to be found in pastoral poetry, beginning in Antiquity and continuing through the Middle Ages and the Renaissance. The scene might have been laid and the speaker presented at the beginning of the poem, and the rest of it might have been the monologue.[6] But Milton chose another, and untraditional, alternative, beginning with the monologue and appending the scene and speaker.[7]

6. As in Theocritus 18 or 21 (*The Greek Bucolic Poets*, Loeb Library, ed. J. M. Edmonds, London, 1912), and elsewhere.

7. A third alternative is possible: the setting may come both at the beginning and at the end of the poem, with the monologue in the middle. (See, e.g., "Januarye" in Spenser's *The Shepheardes Calender*). There are of course myriad instances of setting-monologue and setting-monologue-setting; but "Lycidas" is the only poem I know of arranged as monologue-setting.

Doing so, he was able, in effect, to close the poem in a more distinct and serene perspective than would otherwise have been possible. But most importantly, he was able to give a final impression of the poem as performance; emphasizing the fictional nature of the speaker and the duration of the poem performed. Besides, the process we have observed, wherein the secondary time planes are finally reconciled with the primary, is completed and set in perspective by the shift into a past tense, which forms, as it were, a matrix after the fact for the whole poem. The last eight lines, therefore, do not merely hang from the poem, nor do they refer to something new; rather, they serve to bind it up by throwing it into temporal perspective, by reasserting the speaker, and also, at the last, by signaling toward the inevitable but uncertain future arising organically from the past.[8] Everything, including the recapitulation of the day and the final gesture of the speaker, works toward the fullness and serenity with which the poem closes. We are left with a rich double sense of finality and continuance.

It is easier now to see the ways in which the time scheme of "Lycidas" differs from that of the "Polifemo" and the "Nativity Ode." We find very little resembling rapid alternation of tenses. The time scheme of "Lycidas" seems more dependent on other elements in the poem; movement in time, for example, cannot be seen clearly in the mere change of tense, but has to be gauged also by close attention to the sense. There seems to be less violence in the process of reconciling tenses. All such contrasts have, doubtless, something to do with the difference in subject matter and the relative importance of other elements in the poems.

In analyzing "Lycidas" from the point of view of time, it is necessary to speak of time planes rather than tenses alone; for the movement of the poem is clearly in terms of closer divisions. In brief, we might conveniently summarize the time planes as follows: (1) present (speaker's perform-

8. We must avoid the temptation to speculate biographically: see below, note 9.

ance), (2) remote past (speaker and Lycidas' youth), (3) less
remote past (Lycidas' death), (4) recent past (procession of
"mourners"), (5) present (flower passage), and (6) new
present (Lycidas risen). Though such a scheme as this cannot but distort somewhat, it has the advantage of showing
clearly the dynamic structure of the poem. Throughout the
poem we are not allowed to lose sight of the speaker's present (1); in fact, certain otherwise jarring changes in tense
could be well explained as reassertions of this, the primary
time plane. It forms a steady line toward which the other
secondary time planes seem in their succession to ascend. We
have seen how they (2 to 5) follow progressively one upon
the other, to the point (with 5) of actual merging. Once the
merging has been achieved, the poem does not merely remain static; it leads to a new present which is established
with the announcement that Lycidas is risen. Finally, the
new present itself, which grew in the process of the poem
from the speaker's original present, is put in perspective by
the last eight lines; they are, therefore, best described as
creating a time matrix for the whole poem rather than a
time plane.

The dominance of the speaker's present is closely bound
up with an important aspect of the poem which has already
received some notice, the poem as performance. From the
very first ("Yet once more . . . I come") the reader is made
to consider the poem as sung by the speaker. Since the speaker
undertakes to perform the poem, he must justify his presump-
tion, balancing modest disclaimers with proofs of his fitness
("Who would not sing for Lycidas?"; "For we were nurst
upon the self-same hill"; etc.). Under such a light, we have
no trouble seeing the justness of the speaker's references to
himself; they harmonize with one of the most striking elements of the poem, the characterization of the speaker, and
with the ceremonial function he sets out to perform.[9] Be-

9. When the poem is interpreted as biographical evidence or when the
speaker is identified with John Milton, there seems to be a tendency to judge

sides, the speaker's personal reference to the remote past when he was Lycidas' companion provides a kind of link between the speaker's present time plane and that of the remote past, foreshadowing the way the movement of the poem will eventually reconcile the two. Other instances of the speaker's characterization and peculiar function were cited in the analysis, and their close relation to the time scheme was shown. It remains to stress once again the forceful manner in which the last eight lines complete the impression of the poem as process and performance, and reassert the character of the speaker.

The space required for working out the poem as performance and for evolving the time scheme is a major source of tension; for it allows the detailed elaboration of the causes for grief, and the gradual intensification of what seems hopelessness. The flower passage has the effect almost of stalling. As the speaker himself says,

> For so to interpose a little ease,
> Let our frail thoughts *dally* with false surmise.

Up to this point in the poem there has been a concentration on the completely negative aspects of death: absence from earthly existence and decay of the body. Throughout the

---

the personal references as egotistical. E. M. W. Tillyard tells us that the poem begins with "characteristic egotism" (*Milton*, New York, 1930, p. 83). He goes on to interpret "Lycidas" as a document illustrating Milton's "spiritual development" (see especially p. 85). Leaving aside the delicate question of the value of imaginative works as biographical evidence, we should note that nothing has been said about the fictional speaker. Actually most of the elements potentially egotistical serve the necessary purpose of characterizing the speaker, realizing the poem as performance, and explaining the speaker's fitness, his right to mourn for Lycidas. Douglas Bush also interprets the poem biographically, but counters the charge of egotism by asserting that "Milton's personal struggle becomes universal" (*English Literature in the Earlier Seventeenth Century*, pp. 306–68). For us, since we are not concerned with Milton's life, the important thing is the characterization of the fictional speaker; and *he* can hardly be called egotistical.

major part of the poem, the poet is interested in maintaining such a concentration; that is, in presenting a pagan conception of death, its noble as well as its hopeless side. Early in the poem the qualms of the speaker in continuing to cultivate the muse (lines 64–66 ff.) are answered only in pagan terms: the nearest approach to survival after death is through "fame"; as *Jove* "pronounces lastly on each deed, / Of so much fame in Heav'n expect thy meed." The emphasis, though sometimes blurred by commentators' well-meaning attempts to Christianize the pagan elements, falls upon the words "Jove" and "fame." [10] It might be said that the two words are ambiguous in that they imply the Christian God and actual immortality of the soul. But we may say in reply that they do not do so necessarily; that they seem rather to derive directly from the usual practice of pagan poets; and that, if they did suggest Christian counterparts, if the whole Christian scheme of reward and salvation were set forth so early in the poem, the poet would have sprung too soon the mainspring of his poetic structure. We are not only unwarranted in making substitutions; we can do actual damage to the best reading. As far as the flower passage, then, we find no alternative to the total loss of Lycidas, even the loss of his body; not only has he died, but he has also suffered the horrible fate, in pagan terms, of having died in the ocean where his body and (by temporary pagan implication) his spirit can find no rest (lines 12–14):

> He must not float upon his wat'ry bier
> Unwept, and welter to the parching wind,
> Without the meed of some melodious tear.

All the same, even with such a tear, he *must* "float upon his wat'ry bier," and *must* "welter to the parching wind." Later, after the flower passage, the poignancy returns intensified (lines 154–55):

10. See, for example, Hughes' edition, p. 289, note to lines 81–84, which he calls "essentially Christian."

> Whilst thee the shores, and sounding Seas
> Wash far away, where'er thy bones are hurl'd . . .

The only solace is indirect or fanciful, but still ineffectual (lines 163–64):

> Look homeward Angel now, and melt with ruth:
> And, O ye Dolphins, waft the hapless youth.

But finally the resolution comes, and it comes suddenly in Christian terms:

> Weep no more, woeful Shepherds weep no more,
> For Lycidas your sorrow is not dead
>
> .   .   .   .
>
> So Lycidas, sunk low, but mounted high,
> Through the dear might of him that walk'd the waves . . .

Here we find what I have already called the central paradox of the poem. Is it not, we must ask ourselves, a mere commonplace that the body sinks but the spirit rises? Is the poem not merely switching from a pagan to a Christian conception of death? Certainly we would have to admit that the central paradox, extracted from the poem, states a platitude. Yet it is gradually and dramatically prepared for in the poem; and in terms of the poem it is not a flat statement but rather something artistically achieved. Even the best Christian has doubts; he is cut off from any empirical knowledge of death and so is not immune to speculation on the possibility of no immortality. The whole emphasis of the major part of the poem is on the personal loss and the inability to render direct homage to the body of the dead man. The poet is not interested in making a flat unconnected statement; he presents the evolution of an attitude. In terms of structure, and particularly in terms of the time scheme, the process of evolving the attitude is, of course, crucially important. However commonplace the central paradox may seem by itself, in the poem it is vital and pivotal; for it fulfills the time scheme, links pagan and Christian elements, and, we shall see later, completes an evolution of attitude. Thus all the aspects of the poem, including our present main concern, the time scheme, contribute to its gradual process, to the elaboration of its structure.

6. Summary

That special uses of time exist in the Baroque lyric seems reasonably certain. We can generically describe them as having to do with narrated time and with the whole structure of a poem. Other possible uses, having to do with narrative time and with only a part of the structure of a poem, have been neglected on a priori and empirical grounds as insignificant. Simple patterns of the sort we are considering may be found in a variety of forms in the major European literatures of the Baroque age: in particular, retrogressive, progressive, and circular. Not all possibilities could, of course, be exhausted in a catalogue of simple time patterns. In fact, the longer analyses revealed, in several of the major Baroque poetic achievements, complex patterns that may well be characteristic only of the poems in which they exist. In the "Nativity Ode" the tenses and time references establish two time planes, past and present, and by means of a gradual and intricate process work toward their identification in a new present.

Another kind of oscillation was found in the "Polifemo." Here it was more radical and permanent. The pattern was achieved largely by means of accelerating and diminishing the oscillation. Toward the end there was no resolution on a higher level: the original alternation between past and present continues throughout the poem, so that identification of the two time planes comes about not as the result of a process of reconciliation but rather as the result (or in mathematical terms the limit) of an ever more rapid and closely contested struggle between the two tenses. Identification is achieved through a kind of stalemate.

In "Lycidas" the time pattern is still more involved. There is a main time plane in the present tense, toward which the lesser time planes, in the course of the poem, move gradually from the remote past to a present that consolidates itself with the present of the main time plane. Each of the three poems, then, offers a special time pattern—so special that it would not be profitable or accurate to reduce the first two poems to, say, the class of alternating patterns, and the last to the class of progressive patterns.

In each poem the time pattern is general and complex enough to constitute what I have called the time structure. And, again, in each poem the time structure is important enough to constitute a principal element of the main structure. It has been assumed all along that the time structure has no independent existence apart from the whole meaning of the poem. It has therefore been analyzed only to be fitted back into place. In each instance not only did the time structure not conflict with the sense, it actually supported and enhanced it. Whatever the faults of the poems may be, articulation of structural elements is not one of them. In the "Nativity Ode" the major phases of the development of the time structure coincide with those of the thematic development. Though in the "Polifemo" the coincidence is less obvious, it nevertheless exists. As the dénouement is being prepared for, the tense oscillates and there are three evenly spaced sections of from six to eight stanzas in the present tense which mark three main phases in the action: Galatea's plight, the coming of Acis, and the sudden appearance and harangue of Polyphemus; as the dénouement actually takes place, the final violent act of Polyphemus and its consequence, the tense oscillates with ever increasing rapidity. In "Lycidas" the gradual process of reconciling the movement of tenses from the remote past with the main time plane helps in the necessary prolongation of desperate grief. The new present is established in time for the climax of the poem. In all three poems, then, every major element of structure, including time, is integrated into the whole.

In "Lycidas" there is a particularly happy coincidence. As it happens, the central paradox of the poem, the explicit version of it, occurs along with the full establishment of the "temporal paradox," by which I mean what might be called the contradictory reconciliation of time planes that occurs in the poem. The present of Lycidas dead becomes identified with the speaker's present, and the identification verges into the new present of Lycidas risen. In the other two poems, paradox also plays a large part. The temporal paradox in the "Nativity Ode" is, so to speak, coextensive with the central paradox: both are involved in earning the identity of the day of Christ's birth and Christmas 1629 (or, for that matter, 1960). Likewise, in the "Polifemo" the pervading paradox consists in the existence of the action simultaneously in two time planes. It is not possible to generalize and say that paradox exists wherever time is a conspicuous and dominant source of structure. But it is possible to say so about the poems analyzed, and about any poem whose time structure is evolved through the process of identifying or reconciling time planes. In such poems the paradox is fundamentally a result of the coexistence of the *einmalig* and the *stetig*. A single action which, according to common sense, took place at a more or less definite time in the past is set open to the possibility of recurring indefinitely. In a sense, the birth of Christ occurs every Christmas. Acis and Galatea are always trying to escape the jealous violence of Polyphemus. And mourning for Lycidas may, any number of times, be conducted in the same manner. Constructing such a paradox is a means of conquering time through time.

Another notable feature of the elaboration of time structure in the three poems is the gradual or continuous way in which transitions are made. In the several analyses we have seen how a progressive or a past indefinite tense or a participle or a subordinate clause supported a transition from one main tense to another in such fashion as to avoid a flat contradiction. In larger terms, the tendency can be related to the gradualness and minuteness with which actions are described or reasonings unfolded. A good example is Crashaw's "Musicks Duell." The tendency is related also to the kind of gradual change of speaker's attitude which occurs in a poem like Donne's "The Sunne Rising" (from "Busy old fool, unruly sun" to "Shine here to us, and thou art everywhere"): the subject of the second half of my study. And finally, in very general terms, the tendency can be related to the greater emphasis on the mode of presentation, rather than the thing presented.

Although it is certainly wise to avoid viewing the Baroque age as a literary Counter Reformation, the use of time, with its implications in paradox and gradual continuity, may be linked to prevailing Christian doctrines. The Christian view of time as bounded at either end made possible a heightened awareness of the simultaneity of all events, past, present, and future. A fundamental paradox results from the double view of time, under a finite and under an infinite aspect. Let us carry the development a step further: If all events may be considered simultaneous, "finite time" need not be strictly observed according to our empirically chronological habit. A poet could therefore seize upon time as just another contingent and manipulatable element of structure. It may be objected that no Baroque poet stuck consistently to such an extremely relativistic formulation; yet the "Nativity Ode," for instance, lies quite a distance from the usual Renaissance lyric along the continuum which stretches to a terminus in radical Apollinaire. Again, it may be objected that the Christian view of time has from the beginning been essentially the same, and that it must be explained to what degree its particular use in the Baroque lyric is a novelty. Historical considerations may be urged. What had previously been taken for granted as a given postulate of experience received, in the dissolution of the Scholastic world-view, a kind of re-evaluation and a closer focus than before. Besides, the crumbling of the old world-view made it necessary for the poet, in writing a complex lyric, to cope with uncertainty by including more explicit signs of a strengthened and structured outlook. It is probably for such reasons that although some concern for time is evident from Antiquity, the conspicuous use of time as a means of structure in the lyric is a development of the Baroque age. Still, it would be a mistake not to keep a clear distinction between the Christian view of time and the poetic use we have seen time put to. In practice, Christian doctrine would insist on strict chronology and the reality of time, whereas the Baroque poet freely laid distorting stresses and even verged on making time unreal. Likewise, it would be a mistake to confuse either assertions about time or doctrinal background with the actual use of time in the text. Yet it remains true that the poetic use of time can be related to tendencies in Christian teaching, such as chiliasm and contemplation (in the tradition of spiritual exercises), which in effect work toward a depreciation of time, and even an escape from it.

Assuming, then, that there are never any clean breaks in human history, we need not be disturbed by the persistence of traditional elements. Our difference lies in degrees of emphasis. Moreover, we do not have to believe that the advanced currents of intellectual history are necessarily the ones that directly influence the structure of poetry. It is, for example, possible to speak of Protestant poetry and Catholic poetry during the Renaissance, but do the two categories have to do with structure or merely with subject matter? We find ourselves dealing perhaps with imponderables. The best we can do is to look around, after determining characteristics of style, and choose among trends of the time those that seem related to what we have observed in poetry. Certainly, as I have suggested, the challenging of the old religious orthodoxy was one such trend. Another would be the new prominence given time in the scientific challenge to Aristotelian physics. St. Thomas dealt with time by dividing it into *tempus, aevum,* and *aeternitas,* designating the modes of perception of flesh-and-soul creatures, disembodied souls, and celestial beings. Man was thus set in a definite temporal scheme, in which what really mattered was not abstract time but rather potentiality and actuality. In Galileo, however, time took on a new importance as the measure of motion or change: this importance consisted largely in the fact that motion or change was no longer thought to be an unsightly imperfection but rather a glory and chief attribute of the universe. Since disembodied souls and celestial beings were completely left out of the picture, time, along with space, became a mathematically manipulatable absolute. Newton went further and distinguished between absolute and relative time, thus theoretically freeing the scientific notion from our empirical perception. It may well be that the phenomena we observe in poetic structure are related to the extraordinary and radical prominence given to time in the Baroque age.[1]

Analysis of time structure is a useful, though limited, aid

1. In pursuing a study of time in science and poetry in the Baroque age, one would begin with E. A. Burtt, *The Metaphysical Foundations of Modern Physical Science* (New York, 1927), and go on with such works as J. A. Gunn, *The Problem of Time: An Historical and Critical Study* (London, 1929), L. R. Heath, *The Concept of Time* (Chicago, 1936), J. Sivadjian, *Le Temps: étude philosophique, physiologique et psychologique* (Paris, 1938), W. Gent, *Die Philosophie des Raumes und der Zeit* (Bonn, 1926), and M. Bense, *Konturen einer Geistesgeschichte der Mathematik: Die Mathematik in der Kunst* (Hamburg, 1949), Vol. 2.

to our understanding of an individual poem. The next step is to explore the possibility of making significant generalizations about the importance of conspicuous time structure to a characterization of Baroque style as a whole. To do so it is necessary first to assume that Baroque style as a whole does exist, and then to prove the assumption. The proof would consist in establishing chronologically the novelty and prevalence of particular forms of stylistic elements in, for the present purpose, the Baroque lyric. At the very start it must be decided whether the whole mass of poetry written in the Baroque period should be accounted for, or whether evidence should be sought principally in the great works. Certainly, in order to define the new style one should begin with the great works and use the lesser to illustrate and confirm. The word "great" itself needs exhaustive definition. It is possible that "greatness" (along with prevalence and novelty) belongs to Milton and the Metaphysicals rather than to Ben Jonson, to Góngora and Quevedo rather than to the Argensola brothers, to Marino rather than to Chiabrera. In France and Germany, where poetic greatness is less evident, the contest is closer between, say, Théophile and Malherbe or Gryphius and Opitz. Yet even in the so-called classical poets, traits of the dominant style of the period can be discovered. In fact, an approach to the dominant style can be made through them, as also through the bulk of traditional Renaissance poetry—pastoral, anacreontic, amatory—which continued to be written in the seventeenth century. But on the whole, it would be unprofitable in the present context to labor through minor poetry and occasional verse, of which great quantities were produced, merely to show that it is neither great nor representative; there is no reason to avoid a characterization of Baroque poetic style which would not directly apply to it. The same problem is present in other periods. Would it be necessary in defining Wordsworth's poetic style to account for the tremendous number of trivial and occasional pieces? Could neoclassic style be profitably compared with romantic style on the basis of the occasional verse written in each period?

It should be sufficient, then, to have demonstrated a widespread awareness of time as contingent and manipulatable and as a start to have shown that time was used structurally in poetic achievements as great or as representative as those of Milton, Góngora, Donne, and others. With respect to the Renaissance and Middle Ages, the poems fulfill the condition of being novel in possessing significant time structure. By their intrinsic merits and their extrinsic influence they fulfill the condition of being prevalent. Further studies might explore the whole works of particular authors in an attempt to show their development and achievement in the use of time structure. It would be possible, for example, to make generalizations about the works of Vaughan and Quevedo and Kuhlmann and many others, and with the structural use of time well established as a major element of Baroque poetic style, to see other traits in proper perspective. The sort of endless enumeration and loose monolinear development that vitiates so much of especially German, French, and Italian poetry of the period could be clearly seen as a survival of the medieval and Renaissance practice of *amplificatio*.[2] Also, the undercurrent of traditional practice inherited from the Renaissance and hardly transformed, could be more accurately appraised. Perhaps in time it will be possible to speak of period styles, Baroque in particular, with some degree of descriptive accuracy and basic unanimity. Meanwhile it should help to see the Baroque lyric in another phase and get a new triangulation.

2. The concept was borrowed by medieval rhetoricians (Geoffroi de Vinsauf, for instance) from classical treatises on rhetoric. Originally it signified nothing more than the rhetorical means of emphasizing or clarifying a thought. But in the Middle Ages it came to signify the means whereby discourse may be prolonged; it was used to indicate the stereotyped patterns which might serve as crutches for letter writers (*ars dictandi*), sermon writers, and, alas, poets. See Edmond Faral, *Les Arts poétiques du XIIe et du XIIIe siècle*, Paris, 1924.

III. DRAMA AS A MEANS OF STRUCTURE

7. The Uses of Drama

Another approach, universally applicable, which reveals essential characteristics of Baroque poetry is analysis of the rhetorical situation in a poem. At first glance the possibilities may not seem greatly significant. In fact, if we consider the enormous quantity of traditional poetry, sonnets, pastorals, and songs which continued to be written throughout the sixteenth and seventeenth centuries, we may despair of reaching any significant conclusions at all. It is again necessary to speak of innovation rather than common practice. For in every poem the rhetorical structure is at bottom the same. It is determined by a basic situation: the interrelation of speaker, audience (persons or other entities addressed either directly or implicitly), and reader. There are, inevitably, drawbacks to such a comprehensive scheme. Where is the speaker in a dialogue poem like Samuel Daniel's "Ulysses and the Siren"? Indeed, where is the audience? It could be insisted, perhaps justly, that the poem is a dramatic dialogue and by its very nature implies no one speaker. Still, the conflict of viewpoints and the final resolution, all within the unity of the poem, suggest a unifying attitude which guides the whole procedure. For our purposes we could think of a speaker assuming masks, alternately impersonating the Siren and Ulysses. It is less easy to assume that an audience exists. One possibility, not very convincing, is to say that the audience consists in the ethical problem to which the speaker addresses himself. In other words, audience and subject matter are collapsed together. Perhaps more convincingly, it may be said that Ulysses and the Siren become the audience alternately; when one is the audience the other is the speaker. Although such arguments may seem tenuous, they serve to reinforce a significant fact about lyric poetry: that the most complex rhetorical situation to be found in poetry may be analyzed in terms of speaker, audience, and reader, and that poems that seem to lack one or two "members" may be considered limiting cases. We may go further and say that the highest order of complexity possible in the lyric depends upon preventing the full rhetorical situation from collapsing. In other words, poems are more complex the more fully they make use of the whole rhetorical situation.

So simple an account should be elaborately qualified. One would have to discuss the objections of those who might say that in some poems there is no one speaker, no one audience, no one reader. Yet, in reply, each rhetorical member of a poem has its own set of complexities. The speaker's attitude may change. His area of awareness or information may expand and contract. But the "inconsistencies" are still part of a full characterization of the speaker. If they are too violent, the poem suffers; its unity is impaired.

The notion of audience is more difficult. First of all, the word may be said not to admit of a specialized use. And it may be too easily confused with the third rhetorical member, the reader. I would plead the want of a better term. As for the concept, the most serious objection is that in many poems it seems not to exist. In a poem like the "Polifemo" (not counting the Dedication) the speaker himself does not directly address any characters or other entities within the poem. The same would be true of all poems in which the speaker refers to entities not in the second person but consistently in the third. By way of solution it might be held either that the audience is indistinguishable from the subject matter or that the audience and the reader are identified. In terms of the total rhetorical situation, there is an important and obvious similarity between second-person and third-person audiences: both are defined by the subject matter and the speaker's attitude. We have some excuse, then, for widening the meaning of audience. The difficulty is, in the end, mainly terminological. As for the third rhetorical member, the reader, no troublesome inconsistencies seem to lie in the concept: all poetry needs to be communicated. Different poems demand different qualifications: a reader may be called upon to sympathize or oppose, to eavesdrop or discuss; and his role need not remain constant but may vary. A poem has the right to assume an omnicompetent reader, who can enter into the fiction and become a lover, a devotee, a Christian; who, in short, is able and willing to assume whatever mask is called for. We may say, then, that the reader is always a double figure, both totally aware and also capable of playing the role assigned him. All poems demand the same omnicompetence from their reader; but they differ in the particular roles they assign. The concept of reader should therefore be large enough to include both aspects of the reader's task. What matters most in criticizing individual poems is the particular role of the reader; in practice, then, it is a convenience to restrict the concept of reader to that aspect alone.

We must eventually inquire how the three rhetorical members are interrelated. In general we may say that the audience is characterized, at least in part, by the speaker's attitude toward it; that the speaker's attitude toward the audience characterizes, in turn, the speaker himself; and that the reader is partially characterized by the relationship between speaker and audience. But rhetorical members are not only interrelated, they interact. Since poems communicate themselves in time, the rhetorical situation must be thought of as dynamic. To designate the process of interaction, we may borrow the word "drama"; and to designate the effect, we may coin the word "dramaticality." Ultimately, of course, these words derive from the Greek *drāma,* meaning first an action and then the representation of an action. In the latter sense it came to mean the theatrical performance of an action; and that is the meaning the word commonly has in English. But if we go back to the definition of drama as the representation of an action and take the adjective "dramatic" to signify *like* the representation of an action, then the word dramaticality may be defined as the quality produced by means similar to those used in representing an action. Let us say that a complex action is one that has a beginning, middle, and end and is therefore, if successful, organically evolved as in a play; and also let us allow that the degree of dramaticality is intensified by the complexity within unity of the action. Then, if we broaden the meaning of "complex action" to include the representation of a complex attitude, we can apply the term "dramaticality" to lyric poetry and say that lyric poetry has a high degree of dramaticality when it contains the representation of a complex attitude. In such a way it becomes possible to use the term dramaticality in talking about poetry without restricting its reference to only those features which poems may have in common with plays. Clearly, it is much preferable to the largely pejorative term "theatricality," which has been adduced as a category of Baroque style.

Granted that the rhetorical situation is dynamic, let us try to distinguish meaningfully between two kinds of rhetorical situations: one that remains constant and one that evolves. A poem whose rhetorical situation remains constant begins by announcing its theme and quickly defining its rhetorical members, and then proceeds to elaborate the implications. Relations between the rhetorical members are not changed; they are merely explained. A simple instance of a constant rhetorical situation would be the well-known anonymous sonnet "No me mueve, mi Dios, para quererte." In it the relationship between speaker and audience is set forth essentially in the first main clause, and the rest of the poem only sustains and elaborates it. One may say that the relationship becomes intensified in being explored, but it does not evolve as it does in, for example, Donne's "The Sunne Rising" (see text, below, pages 233–34). A poem whose rhetorical situation evolves is necessarily more complex. It can begin with only a suggestion of its theme and only a provisional relationship between its rhetorical members. In the course of the poem the theme is defined and the provisional relationship modified through refinement or complication. In Donne's poem the attitude of the speaker toward his audience, the sun, is very different at the beginning of the poem from what it is at the end. It is drastically, yet gradually, changed. Certainly, the distinction between elaborated and evolved rhetorical situations cannot always be made so clearly as between the Spanish sonnet and "The Sunne Rising." Still, it proves to be a significant and useful distinction.

In few words, the rhetorical situation may be defined as the complex and dynamic relationship between speaker, audience, and reader. One may isolate a single rhetorical member for the purposes of analysis. One may describe the speaker's attitude toward his audience, or characterize each of the rhetorical members. But the isolated elements have their full meaning only when they are reintegrated into the whole rhetorical system of the poem and seen as part of the drama. The process of isolating rhetorical members is by no means simple. All the elements of a poem are so mutually dependent, so interpenetrated, that no one can dispense with the others. It is therefore difficult to answer the question of exactly what elements contribute to defining the rhetorical situation and what elements do not; and perhaps it is impossible to make any rigorous theoretical classification. But what I call the rhetorical members are undoubtedly of central importance. Other elements, of rather less importance, may contribute notably to the dramaticality of a poem. We might call them "devices," and single out those most characteristic of Baroque practice: modes of discourse, such as assertions, questions, and exclamations; particularization of time and place; repetition and emphasis; and, for want of a better expression, taking the opposite or alternative into account. Rather than go on to discuss imagery or metrical form, both of them subjects for long study, I shall confine my scope to these devices, and then proceed to extended analyses in terms of the total rhetorical situation.

It is quite possible for a poem to be written exclusively in one mode of discourse. Certainly there are poems consisting of nothing but assertions, and one may come upon poems that are nothing but series of questions or exclamations. For the most part, however, poetry in every age has used all three modes of discourse. Assertions have included quotations and images; questions have been direct and rhetorical; exclamations have been general and specific. Generalizations concerning the use of modes of discourse in any one style would be hazardous. Yet in the poems to be analyzed, and generally in Baroque poetry, there is a tendency which can often be described in terms of the modes of discourse: a tendency toward particularization, toward sharp definition of an evolving rhetorical situation.

Questions and exclamations derive from their form a special meaning which they would not have if recast as assertions.[1] That meaning is difficult to describe in abstract terms; but it is nonetheless discernible. That the speaker of the *Aeneid*, for example, says "tantaene animis caelestibus irae?" in the form of a question, is significant for the speaker's characterization. The degree of significance is parallel to the de-

---

1. The remarks in "Longinus" on the effect of questions, as distinct from assertions, are theoretically suggestive, though not historically influential. See *On the Sublime*, 18. Much also is of interest in the discussions of asyndeton (19–21), hyperbaton (22), and hyperbole (38).

gree of difference (leaving prosody out of account) between the question as it is found and as it might be rephrased in the form of an assertion: "tantae animis caelestibus irae." As a question, the words contribute toward defining an attitude of the speaker and also toward defining the relationship between speaker and reader. In the present instance, the speaker's attitude is one of cautious respect or incredulity; at all events, it shies away from a direct condemnation of Juno. Furthermore, the very fact that the reader is addressed in the form of a question suggests a dependent relationship between speaker and reader—that is, a relationship more complex and particular than the relationship suggested by the words not as question but as assertion.

Exclamations may be considered in the same light, for both modes of discourse possess certain effects in common. Both characterize the speaker beyond the power of the same words as assertion, and both suggest a more complex and particular relationship between the speaker and the other rhetorical members. Moreover, they both produce an effect of immediacy, creating an expectant attitude in the reader. Again, we can measure the degree of characterization or immediacy by rendering an exclamation into an assertion. Compare "How vainly men themselves amaze / To win the Palm, the Oke, or Bayes . . ." [2] with "Men vainly do themselves amaze . . ." Disregarding the clumsiness of the reworking, we may observe how the change in mode, from exclamation to assertion, makes the speaker more aloof from the reader and obviates the need for immediate reaction. Moreover, the reworking is not as multivalent as the original: there are fewer ways in which the assertion can be qualified and evaluated later on, fewer directions in which it can move.

Besides the modes of discourse, other means of defining the rhetorical situation are emphasis, repetition, and particularization. The first two are self-explanatory. Without exhaustive tabulation, the most significant thing one can

2. "The Garden" in Marvell's *Works* ed. Margoliouth, *1*, 48.

say is that they are used conspicuously in Baroque poetry. The third is more important and somewhat harder to express. To give a simple instance, it carries some weight that a rhetorical member be particularized to the extent of being overtly named as, say, a lover, a shepherd, or a poet. True, in a short lyric mere naming of the rhetorical members does not carry the reader very far into the complexities of a good poem. In fact, in much good poety the rhetorical members are not named at all, but must, in effect, be named by the reader. Such poetry rejects one means of particularization in order to achieve greater complexity through suggestiveness. The same is true of the particularization of time and place. Ordinary designations of time and place can be dispensed with in the interest of meaningful ambiguity. All the same, a powerful means of particularization is to designate time and place as precisely as possible. Especially in Baroque poetry one notices a tendency toward hereness and thisness, rather than thereness and thatness. It is all part of a more general trend toward instantaneousness, which we have noted in connection with time structure; the poem becomes more and more a record of change from moment to moment.

The last rhetorical device I would like to consider *in abstracto* is hard to name. It consists in a sort of negative definition that achieves precision by examining the alternatives or by taking the opposite into account. In simplest form it is a negative statement: "Sweetest love, I do not goe, / For weariness of thee . . ." [3] Immediately the two alternatives present themselves to the reader's mind in a more forceful or suggestive way than if the statement had been positive. Negation of this sort is a means of defining or structuring the speaker's character: it leads the reader into a cosmos complicated by the existence of *possible* motives and alternatives. Sometimes the alternatives are not so clear and the reader is not allowed to make a definite choice. In Marino's sonnet "La Trasformazione di Dafne," we find the

3. "Song" in Donne's *Poems* ed. Grierson, *1, *18.

line, "almen, se 'l frutto no, coglie le fronde," referring to
Apollo's predicament upon overtaking a Daphne turned into
a tree.[4] The reader is not told categorically that Apollo *cannot* gather the fruit as well. Although the implication is that
he *probably* could not, there is just the possibility that he
could. At least, the reader's choice is not so definite as in the
first example. A still less definite choice is offered in the
formula, especially dear to Góngora, *A* if not *B*.[5] As a "pure"
example, we might take the following lines,

> . . . húmidas centellas,
> si no ardientes aljófares sudando,
> llegó Acis . . .[6]

The alternatives present themselves. We may suspend our
choice, but the implication is that at least one of the alternatives must be allowed: at least *A*, if not *B*. The important
fact is that the cosmos of the poem permits either way of
viewing what actually happened. To that extent the cosmos
is particularized. Variations of the simple formula weight
the choice one way or the other:

> . . . de sitio mejorada, atenta mira,
> en la disposición robusta, aquello
> que, si por lo süave no la admira,
> es fuerza que la admire por lo bello.[7]

It is possible that Galatea admire Acis' lineaments for their
smoothness; but, by implication, she cannot avoid admiring

4. Text in Marino, *Poesie varie* ed. Croce, p. 175. "Frutto" is of course
metaphorical as well as literal and refers also to Daphne in human form.

5. For the formula see Dámaso Alonso, *Evolución de la sintaxis de Góngora*
(Madrid, 1928), pp. 18–36. On pp. 32–36 Alonso considers the close variations
of the generic formula: A, if B; not B, A; not B, but A. One could also go
further and deal with the many examples of other variations: A rather than
B; less A than B; more A than B; etc.

6. Góngora's "Polifemo" in *Obras completas,* ed. Millé, p. 540.

7. Góngora's "Polifemo" in *Obras completas,* ed. Millé, p. 542. As before,
I have slightly altered the Millés' punctuation.

them for their beauty: the one alternative is possible, the other necessary. Through its very uncertainty, the first alternative expands Galatea's possible scope of "action." Galatea exists in a context where choice is possible. The speaker of the poem cannot vouch for her accepting both alternatives: he merely presents them with their proper degree of obligatoriness. As a consequence, the relationship between speaker and audience is particularized in the sense that the speaker's control over Galatea is defined or limited.

Studying the other variations on the simple formula, we would see how the range of choice is further modified. In the present discussion what is important to notice in the Gongorine formula is the concern with alternatives. The poetic cosmos is broad enough to include at least the possibility that an assertion is not wholly true or that its negation may not be false. Góngora's poetry, being particularly rich in the formula and its variations, runs the risk of vagueness or indeterminacy. Yet, when not used to excess, the formula can be, as I have tried to suggest, a source of complexity and particularization.

An even more radical way of expanding and structuring the poetic cosmos can be found in Baroque poetry: allowing something to be several things at once. The poet is not content with one transformation into metaphor, but must offer two or more. All the transformations have equal claim; there is no implied hierarchy as in the formula *A* if not *B*. A good example is to be found at the beginning of the "Polifemo." [8] Polyphemus' cave for him

> bárbara choza es, albergue umbrío,
> y redil espacioso . . .

It is not more one thing than another. It is all three. In different words, the same object is viewed almost simultaneously from three distinct perspectives. Somewhat indirectly the

---

8. In *Obras completas,* ed. Millé, p. 536.

same thing occurs in, for example, Donne's "The Canonization."

> Call us what you will, wee are made such by love;
>   Call her one, mee another flye,
> We'are Tapers too, and at our owne cost die,
>   And wee in us finde the'Eagle and the Dove.
>   The Phoenix riddle hath more wit
>   By us, we two being one, are it.

The rhetorical situation is, of course, more complex than in
the passage from Góngora; but here, as there, the several
metaphors are allowed to exist, as it were, simultaneously,
and no one is permitted to supplant the others. It is quite
possible that the use of multiple metaphors bring about
chaos in a poem. In much German poetry of the Baroque
age there is a notable tendency to string alternate metaphors
together at such length that, apart from sequence, there is no
unified order. The lesson to be drawn is that multiple perspective on one object must be limited and controlled; otherwise it lapses from complexity into chaos.

In a number of Baroque poems we can discern the same
tendency, in terms of total structure, to take into account
alternatives or opposites. Certainly, one might consider in
that light the reconciliation of time planes to be found in the
"Nativity Ode" and "Lycidas." In the first poem the possibility that Christmas is "now" presents itself as an alternative to the historical event. The major part of "Lycidas" is
concerned with the horrible alternative (or opposite) to
what, at the end, is asserted to have "really" happened.[9] In a

9. I refer to the two views of death, pagan and Christian. In pagan terms
the only immortality is "fame." But in Christian terms what "really" happened is that Lycidas was taken into heaven. For other instances of retarded
resolution, taking the opposite into account at length, see Crashaw's "Upon
the Death of Mr. Herrys" and Vaughan's "I walkt the other day (to spend
my hour)."

sense, then, about four-fifths of the poem is occupied with taking into account the alternatives. Not only is the cosmos of the poem made thereby more complex, but also the final affirmation is in the process "earned." In the "Polifemo" the two alternatives, that the action has occurred in the past and that it is occurring now, offer themselves almost as equals; they are reconciled through the radical means of accelerating alternation. Both alternatives are taken into account; the poetic cosmos is made complex, and also particular in that the possibilities are defined.

To continue would eventually land us in a discussion of poetry's relation to reality or would lead us back circuitously to a reconsideration of time. At all events, the point is clear: that the rhetorical situation is of first importance to a criticism of poetry and that the Baroque lyric may be partially described in terms of it. As for defining the rhetorical situation, it seems impossible to avoid naming its main elements and calling them members. It seems likewise impossible to avoid mentioning lesser elements and calling them devices. Members and devices, therefore, will be in constant view. Their meaning and interrelationship have been abstractly defined as far as necessary. Their relevance I shall try to show in analyzing poems of Gryphius, Marino, Théophile, Donne, and Milton, under the aspect of the rhetorical situation.

8. Poems of Gryphius and Marino

At its best, German Baroque poetry is rich in vivid rhetorical situations. Especially characteristic is the use of questions and exclamations. Whether the poem is addressed to man or God, there is an immediate intensity of focus matched elsewhere only in poets like Donne or George Herbert or Edward Taylor. The danger, not always avoided, is that the poem may fall into bombastic or literal-minded *amplificatio*. Too often the poet relies on the piety of his sentiments and too often he is content merely to name the common Christian symbols without achieving them poetically. Much, therefore, of German Baroque poetry still belongs in the medieval Latin tradition of "practical" devotional verse and psalm paraphrase. But now and then this very practicality led to poetically valuable discoveries. There are signs, as we have seen, of an awareness that time within a poem can be manipulated and, in particular, that an effect of momentaneousness can be achieved. There are signs also of an awareness that the rhetorical situation can be varied and intensified, that ordinary rhetorical devices can be used to that end, and, perhaps in some cases, that attitudes can be evolved as well as elaborated.

It is difficult to generalize and say exactly to what extent attitudes can be said to evolve in the German Baroque lyric. So often a poem of, say, Kuhlmann or Gryphius proceeds only by various means of intensification; one should speak not of evolution but of elaboration. The audience is often so vague in terms of dramaticality (mankind or godhead, for example) that the poem becomes merely a series of moral pronouncements. And often the theme is dealt with in such static terms that the poem never becomes more than a set of examples. All the same, even with those drawbacks, many of Gryphius' poems achieve an intensity and an effect of momentaneousness which allow us to place them in the same Baroque tradition that reached its highest achievement outside of Germany. Poets like Gryphius, Fleming, Kuhlmann, and others made full use of questions, exclamations, repetitions, interruptions, abrupt juxtapositions: most of the minor devices for rendering a poem dramatic. Yet, more often than not, their themes, which mostly concern the relation of the soul to God, impose upon them a static or nondramatic treatment. Take, for instance, Gryphius' sonnet on death: [1]

Was hilfft die gantze welt, mensch! deine stunde schlägt.
    Zwar eh' als du vermeint; doch wer muss nicht erbleichen?
Nun wird die schönheit rauch; nun muss die tugend weichen;
    Nun ist dein adel dunst; die stärcke wird bewegt;
    Hier fällt auf eine bahr, der hut und crone trägt;
Hier feilt die grosse kunst; kein Tagus schützt die reichen.
Man sieht kein alter an; die gantz verstellte leichen
    (O freunde! gute nacht!) wird in den staub gelegt;
Du scheidest gantz allein von hier! Wohin so schnelle?
Diss ist des himmels bahn; die öffnet dir die helle,
    Nach dem der strenge printz sein ernstes urtheil hegt.
Nichts bringst du auf die welt, nichts kanst du mit bekommen;

---

1. From the fourth book of sonnets, number 46: "Der Tod." The text is from H. Palm's edition, *Andreas Gryphius: lyrische Gedichte* (Tübingen, 1884), pp. 155–56.

Der einig augenblick hat, was man hat, genommen;
  Doch zeucht dein werck dir nach. Mensch! deine stunde
  schlägt.

Almost all the common rhetorical devices are present. There
is a great deal of repetition; the first and last lines end with
the same impressive phrase. Both time and place are made
as precise as possible. The verbs, describing widely scattered
actions, are almost all in the present tense. The one exception ("Der einig augenblick hat, was man hat, genommen")
serves to intensify the instantaneousness, since it comes at
the end and refers to the moment when death has become
inevitable; in retrospect it stresses the moment of death. In
fact, both the backward reference and the forward reference
in "Nach dem der strenge printz sein ernstes urtheil hegt"
converge upon the one intense moment of the first part of
the poem. Not only is time made fairly precise, but place is
brought into sharp focus. "Hier" is repeated three times.
And the speaker almost points to a path to heaven: "Diss ist
des himmels bahn." In a rather crude way the opposite is
taken into account: all worldly things pass away, but heaven
receives the true Christian. Most of the rhetorical devices
for vivifying poetry are used in the poem, yet the rhetorical
situation is not highly developed. Both speaker and audience
are vague, hardly characterized; we have no way of knowing
whether the speaker is Death, some omniscient mortal, or
merely the sermonizing poet. His attitude does not undergo
change, but remains that of the stern proclaimer of Christian
doctrine. Neither does the attitude of the audience change;
in fact, the audience is so indefinite—doubtless because of the
universal theme of the poem—that it remains for the most
part uncharacterized.
  If we set Gryphius' sonnet alongside other of his poems [2]
we can easily see that the extraordinary use of rhetorical
devices does distinguish it and them from both Renaissance

2. See, for example, pp. 27–28 in this volume.

poems and the prose sermon. In general we may say that much German Baroque poetry has a kind of elementary dramaticality, but seldom does it approach what could be called an evolution of attitudes. Too often one rhetorical device dominates the poem: repetition, questions, or exclamations. And too often the moral or devotional aspects of a poem are so prominent that the rhetorical situation cannot develop. This should be taken in a limited sense: a poem cannot properly exist as a mere series of moral sentiments; nor can a poem which is merely a set of stanzas on the wounds of Christ or the dolors of Mary be said to realize a complex rhetorical situation. In discussing the German poets further one might point out the frequent occurrence of our rhetorical devices, but generally speaking, the rhetorical situation in German Baroque poetry seems to be no more complex than that of the poem just quoted.

Moving on to Italian Baroque poetry as exemplified in Marino, we find the same general tendency and similar failings. In juxtaposing the two traditions I do not mean to suggest that the one is exclusively devotional and the other exclusively amorous. There are both Italian religious poets and German secular poets of the time. The greater emphasis is still on style and not separable content. But the two tendencies, devotional in German and secular in Italian poetry, are the dominant ones in their respective traditions. It is interesting to see how much they have in common and how they complement each other.

In point of theme the contrast between German devotional poetry and the secular works of Marino could not be greater. So many poems of the German Baroque condemn even the innocent beauties of nature; whereas Marino celebrates in most intimate detail the luxuriance of nature, the beauty of women, and the sensual pleasures of love. The Germans had, for the most part, rejected Petrarch. Their guides were rather the Bible and the Christianized pastoral tradition. Marino and his followers, on the other hand, could hardly escape the influence of Petrarch.[3] However they distorted the Petrarchan love conventions, their imagery derived largely from the *Canzoniere,* and their view of love can be interpreted as a disillusioned, not to say cynical, version of Petrarchan love. In spite of the immense divergence in conclusions drawn, then, the two world-views, in German and Italian Baroque poetry, share a common attitude toward the world as sensual and transient; the one tradition says "turn away," the other says "indulge." On a purely secular level both traditions view the world with *desengaño,* in the light of common day. The question is, of course, beyond our immediate scope. One would have to discuss the imagery of the German poets, which is often taken from sensual and transient objects, or the elaborate conventional artifice of the Italian poets. But it is possible that in the end we could say that the two attitudes toward the world had much in common.

Certainly, if we turn again to consider poetic technique, the two traditions are not so divergent as they may seem at first sight. Taking into consideration only the poetry of Marino and his followers, the predominant line of development, we find a tendency toward dramaticality that goes beyond the old Petrarchan usage and moves at least parallel to the tendency we have found in German devotional poetry of the same period. In both German and Italian Baroque poetry there is also a notable tendency toward taking alternatives into account: heaven implies hell, life death, passion lust, and so on. But the two national traditions diverge somewhat in their use of devices to heighten dramaticality. The German poets, as we have seen, make use of the several rhetorical means for intensifying dramatic effect: questions, exclamations, interruptions, and others. In Marino and his followers the effect is sought more by means of the minute and gradual describing of an action. With the Italians we move closer to one of the central achievements of Baroque poetry.

Comparing a *canzone* of Marino with one of Petrarch's, we

3. There are exceptions on both sides, but the contrast remains.

are immediately struck by the contrast. *Canzoni,* in the Petrarchan tradition, discourse on love: *ragionare* is the technical term. On the other hand, Marino's most characteristic *canzoni* present complete dramatic actions ("Amori Notturni," "Trastulli Estivi") or intense dramatic monologues ("La Lontananza," "La Bella Vedova"). In them the element of *ragionare* is much less prominent than in the Petrarchan *canzone.* As an illustration of Marino's procedure we might look at "Amori Notturni." [4] Though it does not by any means stand on the heights of Baroque achievement in poetic technique, it is characteristic of Marino and shows the direction in which poetic practice was moving.

"Amori Notturni" is concerned with little more than a lover's meeting. What appears to interest the poet is not praise or idealization of the beloved, but rather the successive moments of passion. The poem is all in the first person and in the present tense; and the speaker takes on the double aspect of narrator and lover:

> Quando, stanco dal corso, a Teti in seno
> per trovar posa e pace,
> Febo si corca e 'l dí ne fura e cela . . .
> allor Lilla gentil, l'anima mia,
> de la gelosa madre
> e dal ritroso genitor s'invola.

It is hard to say whether the action is *einmalig* or recurrently *stetig:* whether it is happening as the poem progresses or whether it happens every time Lilla escapes from her parents. At all events, the effect is one of instantaneousness. The speaker describes the tryst moment by moment, quotes the conversation that passes between him and his beloved,

---

4. For the text, see below, pp. 220–23. It is printed in *Marino e i marinisti,* ed. Giuseppe Guido Ferrero (Milan and Naples, 1954), pp. 357–60. Benedetto Croce's text in G. B. Marino, *Poesie varie* (Bari, 1913), is much less accurate. "Amori notturni" was first published in 1602, when the first two parts of *La Lira* came out under the title *Le Rime.*

narrates the rise and fall of passion, and finally ends with a scene of farewell. The attitude of the speaker as narrator, however, does not seem to evolve; it does not even change necessarily. Yet as lover, the speaker goes through a usual cycle of emotions, expectancy, delight, frustration, and satisfaction. More exactly, the speaker, after meeting (as lover) his beloved, describes the first transports in a series of rhetorical questions:

> Giunto al mio ben, chi potria dir gli spessi,
> i lunghi, i molli baci?
> i sospir tronchi? i languidi lamenti?
> Chi può contar degli amorosi amplessi
> le catene tenaci?
> gli accesi sguardi? gl'interrotti accenti?
> gli atti dolci e furtivi?
> gli atti dolci e lascivi?

As the transports subside, the speaker begins to talk at length about his love. He directly quotes himself. Then he quotes his beloved's reply, which, by a common dramatic device, breaks off:

> Quanti doni mi porge,
> misero! e non s'accorge
> ch'io per te sola . . . —e vuol seguir:— . . . mi struggo—;
> ma, mosso dal piacer che 'l cor mi tocca,
> le chiudo allor la sua con la mia bocca.

The speaker then proceeds to describe, in rather full unpetrarchan detail, the course of his passion; after which he becomes impotent and is mocked by his beloved:

> Così mi giaccio, inutil pondo, appresso
> a la mia ninfa amata,
> ch'irride il mio stupor rigido e strano.

Still, the speaker turns not against her but rather against his "parte vile insensata," which he addresses angrily and at length. His anger and his beloved's scorn are not properly resolved in terms of the development of attitudes. What happens is that everything is resolved externally:

> Ed ecco uscir fuor de le rive estreme
> de l'indica pendice
> rapido il sol, da la sua nunzia scorto.

And the lovers turn at once to making their farewells. It is she who speaks:

> Ella, ch'esser veduta ha scorno e teme,
> sospirando mi dice:
> —A Dio, ben rivedrenne, e fia di corto:
> a che tanto affannarte?—
> Poi mi bacia e si parte.

Her words are still chiding and supercilious; but nonetheless the speaker, left alone, makes the usual blissful exclamation:

> Io resto e dico:—Invan per me se' sorto,
> invido sol, ché questa notte oscura
> era a me più che 'l dì lucida e pura!—

And the poem ends with the customary *envoi* addressed to the *canzone*.

In the *envoi* the speaker refers to "le mie vergogne," presumably his failings as a lover. But they are not failings of loyalty or sympathy; they are simply physical failings. In fact the relationship between the two lovers is hardly more than physical. Desire brings them together. Their amity is strained at the decline of potency. The lover puts up no defense against his beloved's mockery. And the whole thing is brought to an end without much anguish by the approach of dawn. The attitudes of both speaker and audience are resolved in terms of the physical: their own lust and the rising of the sun. One notes the beginnings of a dramatically fruitful conflict in attitudes, but it is never properly realized. The

speaker as narrator keeps more or less to the same attitude;
he is like someone describing how he plays a dramatic scene.
But the speaker as lover may be said to go through a series
of changes in attitude, though they are none of them well
delineated or properly reflected in the audience. He experi-
ences joy, lust, anger, and finally satisfaction. One emotion
does not, however, grow out of another; first one thing happens, then another, and another: such is the simple mode of
narration. The result is that at the end there is no complex
resolution of conflicting attitudes but rather the re-establishment of a simple attitude which existed at the beginning.

Despite its shortcomings, particularly its final failure to
realize the rhetorical situation, Marino's poem is moving in
the direction of the great stylistic achievements of the Baroque. The poem is presented as the performance of the
narrator-lover, and as such it is the description of a dramatic
scene. In keeping with its dramatic character, time and place
are elaborately and rather precisely established. We are told
in many ways that it is evening. The meeting place of the
lovers is specified as the "antro che de le 'fate' il nome
prende." Once the place has been made precise, the emphasis
throughout the rest of the poem falls upon time. We are reminded again and again of the passage of time by means of
words like "allora," "poi," "mentre," "alfine," as in phrases
like "Io narro a lei . . . poi dico," or more at length:

> Stanco, non sazio, *alfine* alzo a' begli occhi
> gli occhi tremanti, e *poi*
> da le sue labra il fior de l'alma coglio;
> e, mentre il molle seno avien ch'io tocchi,
> e vo tra' pomi suoi
> scherzando, e mille baci *or* dono *or* toglio . . .

Moreover, the emphatic continuous form of the verb in a
phrase like "vo . . . scherzando" cooperates in creating the
effect of gradualness and the immediate passage of time. By

such means the reader is made aware of the relationship between the two lovers as developing in time. Other devices of defining the rhetorical situation are also to be found: questions, vocatives and exclamations, and direct discourse. In particular, the extensive use of direct discourse, quoted conversation, within the narrative framework of the poem creates the strong impression of a dramatic scene. To some extent the opposite is taken into account. At the beginning the elaborate descriptions of nature in the usual mythological terms suggest heroic love. And in the rest of the poem the excess of sentiment suggests the desperate Petrarchan lover. Still, in spite of the traditional trappings, the poem is concerned with lust rather than love. If we consider as "opposites" or alternatives love and lust, we may say that the one is present, if only through suggestion, and contrasts with the baseness of the other.

In terms of the lovers—that is, the speaker and the audience of the poem—there seems to be no conflict between love and lust. Each has a kind of cynical passivity, a willingness to raise the sluice gates and be carried along in the flood of passion. The relationship between the two lovers, therefore, is all too simple and the possibilities of the rhetorical situation remain inadequately realized. There is a series of changes in the lover's attitude, but we can hardly speak of an evolution of attitude. Such is the failure of the poem, and of practically all the poems Marino wrote. While many of the minor devices for defining the rhetorical situation were at his command, he seems to have been unable to seize upon them and create an evolved complexity of attitudes. Marino's achievement lay rather in the skillful description of gradual action; or, in other words, the composition of poems as performance or drama.

It is instructive to observe that Marino has actually refashioned a Renaissance poem which was formerly attributed to Ariosto but has long since been banished from the canon.[5]

5. The text may be found in Ludovico Ariosto, *Lirica,* ed. Giuseppe Fantini (Bari, 1924), among the "liriche apocrife." See also Abdelkader Salza.

The general situation is the same: two lovers meet clandestinely, but in pseudo-Ariosto they are a conventional shepherd and his "vaga pastorella." Marino follows the same first-person mode of narration and, at a distance, the imagery. But once the lovers are together in pseudo-Ariosto they simply embrace and address each other in alternating stanzas which, in their stilted and static way, remind one of operatic arias. Cupid appears in conventional form, but his presence is perfunctory and undramatic. In its utter flatness the *envoi* is an accurate summation: the *canzone* will show, so the speaker boasts, ". . . che non ebbe unque pastore / di me piú lieto e piú felice, Amore." Though it is perhaps unjust to draw conclusions from a comparison between a bad and a mediocre poem, the difference seems in our context to be symptomatic.

Marino's poem may well remind us of such a poem as Donne's "Elegie XIX: Going to Bed," not merely because of the subject matter but also because of the similarity of rhetorical development.[6] Donne, however, as we shall see in other greater poems, went on to achieve just that rhetorical complexity, that evolution of attitudes, toward which Marino and other poets of the time were verging but which they never attained. In the German poets, as well as in Marino, we have noted a remarkable tendency toward what has been called dramaticality: the use of particular rhetorical devices to effect an impression of instantaneousness or gradualness and ultimately of some rhetorical complexity. Their achievement is demonstrably limited and partial. Before going on to Donne and Milton, who most fully realize the tendency, we may profitably pause to consider the French tradition. In it there are instances of achievement which go beyond the German poets and Marino. Among them is Théophile's poem "La Solitude."

"D'una canzone pastorale attribuita a Lodovico Ariosto e imitata da G. B. Marino," *Giornale storico della letteratura italiana*, 56 (1910), 339–60.

6. See also Thomas Carew's "A Rapture" and Thomas Jordan's "To Leda His Coy Bride on the Bridall Night," for example.

9. Théophile's "La Solitude"

So much of the poetry of Marot and Ronsard, to mention two Renaissance poets, is occasional, being addressed to a particular person or composed for a particular event. The tone is often conversational, even casual. Ronsard's "Hymne de la mort," for example, is written as a sort of epistle to the historian Pierre Paschal. From the start the rhetorical situation is clear:

> On ne scauroit, Paschal, desormais inventer
> Un argument nouveau qui fust bon à chanter,
> Soit haut sur la trompette, ou bas dessus la lyre:
> Aux Ancians la Muse a tout permis de dire,
> Si bien, que plus ne reste à nous autres derniers
> Que le vain desespoir d'ensuyvre les premiers
> Et, sans plus, de bien loing recongnoistre leur trace,
> Faicte au chemin frayé qui conduit sur Parnasse . . .[1]

It is a poem, like so many of Ronsard's lyrics, addressed to a particular audience, implying a rather vague, benevolent reader. The speaker is immediately characterized as a poet,

1. *Oeuvres complètes,* ed. Paul Laumonier (Paris, 1935), *8,* 161–62.

friendly and even confidential: in fact, the greater part of the
poem is, from the start, about the writing of the poem.
Throughout most of it the audience remains Paschal, who
is addressed in the second person.[2] But suddenly, in the midst
of an exceptionally long period, without preparation, the
speaker turns to Death and addresses her in the second person: "car à la verité / Bien peu se sentiroit [the soul] de ta
benignité / (O gratieuse Mort) . . ." For a while the speaker
refers to "nous" (= we mortals), at the very end he narrows
down the rhetorical situation to himself ("moi") and Death
("tu"). The change in audience is rather sudden; one can
hardly speak of evolution in the rhetorical situation. Nor is
the speaker's change evolved, for he too changes his identity
from poet-performer to isolated Christian:

> Quand mon heure viendra, Deesse, je te pris,
> Ne me laisse long temps languir en maladie . . .

That is not to say, necessarily, that the unity of the poem
breaks down. One might say that the final rhetorical situation
is not incompatible with that of the major part of the poem.
And the change is handled skillfully, in that it comes about
in the middle of a long period almost without the reader
realizing it. All the same, one does not find a convincing and
progressive development of attitudes; the changes are sudden and radical. Nor does one find as well developed the
particularly effective rhetorical devices we saw in Italian and
German Baroque poetry: it is again a difference between
conversational and "artificial" use. We must conclude, at all
events, that the unity of the poem derives much more from
theme than from the rhetorical situation.

Historical questions aside, it is illuminating to compare
Ronsard's poem with Foscolo's "Dei sepolcri" (1807). Both
poems exist on several levels: the poem as performance, as

2. At one point, it is true, the audience expands (lines 191–92):
   Quiconques dis cecy, ha, pour Dieu! te souvienne
   Que ton âme n'est pas payenne, mais chrestienne . . .

epistle and as meditation, to name three. But in the "Sepolcri" none of these levels is abandoned. For two-thirds of the poem the speaker is cast in the role of poet-performer and the main audience is Ippolito Pindemonte, to whom the discourse, as epistle, is directed. But in the last third of the poem (beginning with line 213) the speaker expands his role, without changing it, by speaking first in the person of Electra and then in the person of Cassandra. By way of preparation the speaker has already expanded the role of Pindemonte: he is converted from being mostly audience to being an "actual" witness ("d'antichi fatti / Certo udisti suonar dell'Ellesponto / I liti," lines 216–18). The prophecy addressed in the second person to the cypress trees at the end of the poem (lines 279 ff.) does not set up an entirely new audience, since it is part of Cassandra's speech. The speaker and the main audience (Pindemonte) are still, by implication, serving the functions they served in the first part of the poem. But in a sense both become witnesses of Cassandra's prophecy; the prophecy itself, though it "actually" took place before Homer's time, is still to be fulfilled in terms of the speaker (poet-performer) and audience (Pindemonte). Unity, therefore, of a complex sort is possible in an epistolary poem, even through change in the rhetorical situation. The important thing is that the change be evolved. That Ronsard did not achieve complex unity through evolutionary change in the rhetorical situation is not surprising. It seems to be, if not the total discovery, at least the peculiar perfected art of the Baroque.

As a fairly clear and simple example of evolutionary change in the rhetorical situation. Théophile's "La Solitude" recommends itself.[3] Partly its advantages lie in the fact that in

3. The *Oeuvres* of Théophile de Viau were published in 1621 and enlarged between 1623 and 1626; the definitive collection, edited by Georges de Scudéry, appeared in 1632. The text here is that of Jeanne Streicher, *Oeuvres poétiques,* première partie (Geneva and Lille, 1951), pp. 16–23. See below, pp. 224–30.

many ways it is a conventional poem. Lovers meeting in a
solitary wood is hardly a new theme; and the conventional
machinery of nymphs and gods is as old as ancient mythological poetry. Nor are the descriptions of nature out of the ordinary: rivulets, elm trees, nightingales—all the usual stage
properties. The first thirteen stanzas are devoted to a description of the forest. But even here there are certain details
to enliven the convention. In fact, the first two stanzas are
more promising than they seem at first glance:

> Dans ce val solitaire et sombre
> Le cerf qui brame au bruict de l'eau,
> Panchant ses yeux dans un ruisseau,
> S'amuse à regarder son ombre.
>
> De ceste source une Naïade,
> Tous les soirs ouvre le portail
> De sa demeure de crystal,
> Et nous chante une serenade.

As the poem begins, the speaker is neutral enough; his attitude is subordinated to the description of the deer in the
setting of the valley. And yet the germ of a characterization
of the speaker and the beginning of a closer relationship between speaker and reader are suggested in the demonstrative
adjective "ce." It is not "un val" but "ce val." The tendency
toward precision continues in the second stanza: the naiad
belongs not to "une source" but to "ceste source." As we
read on, we find that our attention, the attention of the
reader, is constantly being focused on particular objects—
particular, that is, to the extent of having "ce" before them:
"ces forests" (stanza 3), "ce grand chesne" (4), "ses [ces?] ormeaux" (5), "ce doux sejour" (6), "ces solitudes" (8), "ceste
forest" (9), and so on. We also find "ce" before persons and
abstractions. At the same time, especially in stanzas 7–10,
we find the adverbs "y" and "icy" repeated with some in-
sistence. The whole tendency is toward particularization and

instantaneousness: object, place, and time are not just any object, place, and time, but those designated. Insofar as the speaker points out particular objects and places and implies a particular time, his relationship with the reader becomes precise. The degree of precision, of course, is limited if only one means is employed. An additional means is at least hinted at in the second stanza: "Et nous chante une serenade." One way of defining a relationship is to name it, and here the speaker refers to a relationship between himself and someone else, simply by using the pronoun "nous." Of course the reader remains uncertain whether it refers to him or to some class to which he does not belong. And his uncertainty is not relieved. Even later in the poem when Corine appears, the reader cannot assume that "nous" referred only to the speaker and his beloved. The pronoun is precise only to a certain degree: it serves its function in emphasizing the relationship between speaker and reader as observers.

In this first part of the poem there is no second-person audience. The main concern is to characterize the forest. It is dark and silent; the haunt of mythological creatures. It is not "profane" (stanza 9), and even Love enters only "par innocence" (stanza 10). The solitude of the forest is inviolate, for mortals do not disturb it by their presence (stanza 8). And yet there are suggestions of unrest and profanation (stanza 5):

> Et les vents battent les rameaux
> D'une amoureuse violence.

Along with the customary nightingale, there are also the osprey, the owl, and the werewolf. Besides, in the mythological past the forest was the scene of violence (stanza 9):

> Ce ne fut point sans la fascher
> Qu'Amour y vint jadis cacher
> Le berger qu'enseignoit Diane.

And the youth Hyacinth found death here at the hands of
Boreas.[4] The solitude and sanctity of the forest, then, are
not absolute, but exist in contrast to possible violence. In
a sense the opposite is taken into account, and the poem derives a certain measure of tension from that fact. So the
main themes of the poem, love and solitude, are first stated
in terms of the forest and its mythological denizens. In the
process, the speaker is further characterized as a mortal
privileged to explore the forest and to divulge its secrets.

With stanza 14 the speaker turns to address the first second-
person audience:

> Saincte forest ma confidente,
> Je jure par le Dieu du jour,
> Que je n'auray jamais amour
> Qui ne te soit toute evidente.

Previously the relationship between the speaker and the
forest had been particularized by the use of the demonstrative adjective; now the forest becomes personified and exists
in a still more direct relationship of "I" and "thou" with
the speaker. In stanza 16 the speaker finally addresses his
specific audience, Corine the beloved. She is brought into
the forest so that the forest, confidante of the speaker, may
know all. Her arrival is momentaneous and particularized
in that the speaker, in his words, reflects her actions and
designates the objects toward which she moves.

> Corine, je te prie approche,
> Couchons nous sur ce tapis vert:
> Et pour estre mieux à couvert,
> Entrons au creux de ceste roche.

Presumably Corine accedes to the speaker's requests, for he
begins to praise her beauty, part by part; first the eyes, then

4. Théophile says Boreas; but some versions of the legend name Zephyrus
as the rival of Apollo and the slayer of Hyacinth. See the article "Hyacinthus"
in *The Oxford Classical Dictionary*.

her face, hair, and mouth. Attention gradually becomes so centered on the beloved that the first audience—the forest or, more generally, nature—is almost forgotten. But not for long: the solitude is not so complete that nature, already personified, cannot "observe" and respond:

> D'un air plein d'amoureuse flame,
> Aux accens de ta douce voix,
> Je voy les fleuves et les bois
> S'embraser comme a faict mon ame.
>
> Si tu moüilles tes doits d'yvoire
> Dans le crystal de ce ruisseau,
> Le Dieu qui loge dans ceste eau
> Aymera s'il en ose boire.

In terms of the tradition, these are conventional exaggerations. All the same, one must remember that this is no ordinary wood; it is one set apart from mortals for gods and demigods, a supernatural wood. As a matter of fact, the speaker actually becomes jealous of nature which acknowledges the beauty of his beloved (stanzas 31 and 32): the consequences of personification are faced to that extent:

> Voys-tu ce tronc et ceste pierre?
> Je croy qu'ils prennent garde à nous,
> Et mon amour devient jaloux
> De ce myrthe et de ce lierre.

In a sense, the speaker's jealousy is the result of an unsuccessful attempt to reconcile the first and second audiences, nature and Corine. It is as if he has gradually realized that the sympathetic response of nature (in the form of rivers, woods and a water god), the reconciliation of nature and Corine, might become a threat to his dominion over her. The supposed solitude of the wood is not enough; it has become personified and therefore intrusive.

At this point it is a problem how the attitudes of the

speaker can be reconciled. He has become somewhat hostile toward nature and her solitude, and less expansive in mediating between nature and Corine and praising their beauties. As it happens, the attitudes of the speaker are reconciled in two ways. In purely practical terms, the speaker commends to his beloved the complete solitude of a cave, away even from the presences of nature. They will still hear the murmuring waters and the singing birds; but there will be no eavesdroppers, not even the winds "qui ne se peuvent taire, / Ne peuvent escouter aussi" (41). Only Love will be present. Nature, therefore, from such a distance, can only be propitious; even personified, she can offer no distracting rivalries.

The second and most important way in which nature and Corine are reconciled, and thus the speaker's conflicting attitudes, is through attributing to Corine certain aspects of nature (stanzas 36, 37):

> Preste moy ton sein pour y boire
> Des odeurs qui m'embasmeront,
> Ainsi mes sens se pasmeront
> Dans les lacs de tes bras d'yvoire.
>
> Je baigneray mes mains folastres
> Dans les ondes de tes cheveux,
> Et ta beauté prendra les voeux
> De mes oeillades idolatres.

She has fragrance that can be drunk, her arms are lakes (a pun), her hair, waves. This is, of course, conventional hyperbole, and yet, though not with complete success, it functions organically in the poem. In the second stanza here quoted ("Je baigneray mes mains folastres / Dans les ondes de tes cheveux") we have the new counterpart of stanza 27 ("Si tu moüilles tes doits d'yvoire / Dans le crystal de ce ruisseau, / Le Dieu qui loge dans ceste eau / Aymera s'il en ose boire"). In the change, Corine has taken the place of nature, and the speaker the place of the one who gives love. In this way, isolation from nature does not mean rejection of it, but rather a *modus vivendi* with it. The lovers retreat from nature, but nature remains about them. In fact, in some respects Corine becomes nature.

Thus, in several ways the speaker's attitude evolves in the course of the poem: his attitude toward solitude, toward the forest, and toward Corine. At first the solitude of the forest is desirable and sufficient. But as the lover's ardor grows, even the mythological presences of the forest become intrusive, and the lover seeks greater isolation. At the same time the speaker's attitude toward the forest undergoes a change. Though the forest is not "profane" (9) but "saincte" (14), it harbors suggestions of violence and, in the lover's mind, offers reasons for jealousy. Finally the speaker is reconciled to it by retiring as much as possible from it. As for Corine, the speaker's attitude toward her evolves in terms of solitude and the forest. At first she is addressed as a newcomer who must be introduced to the various creatures of nature. But gradually the speaker concentrates his attention upon her alone. In a sense, she begins by viewing solitary nature and ends by extending it and finally in part becoming it.

Other elements of the poem contribute to the general effect. At first the mode of discourse is almost wholly assertive. Then in the catalogue of Corine's beauty (mostly stanzas 19 to 24) exclamations appear. And from stanza 32 to the end, exclamations and questions succeed one another more thickly, as the speaker demands more and more an immediate response from Corine: "Voys-tu ce tronc et ceste pierre?" . . . "Sus ma Corine que je cueille" . . . "voy" . . . "Oy" . . . "Vois" . . . "Oy" . . . "Approche, approche ma Driade" . . . "Ne crains rien, Cupidon nous garde, / Mon petit Ange es tu pas mien?" . . . "Ha!" . . . "Dieux

que ceste façon timide / Est puissante sur mes esprits!"
. . . "Ma Corine que je t'embrasse" . . . "Voy" . . . It is
an effect of momentaneousness and concentration. By implication Corine accedes to the speaker's demands; his successive exhortations and questions are a moment to moment
record of her actions. All the while, the same sort of localization we noticed at the beginning of the poem continues in
the repetition of "ce" and "icy." Just when the union of the
lovers has been achieved ("Ma Corine que je t'embrasse"),
the speaker, having in every way reached his goal, is able to
look at himself and Corine objectively in terms of the winds:

> Les vents qui ne se peuvent taire,
> Ne peuvent escouter aussi,
> Et ce que nous ferons icy
> Leur est un incogneu mystere.

All the strands are gathered together: time has been focused
on the immediate present and can look to the future; the
attitudes of the speaker (and indirectly the attitudes of
Corine and the reader) have evolved to a fairly complex
stability.

Because there is so much plot to it, one is tempted to
think of "La Solitude" as a narrative lyric and contrast it
with its namesake by Saint-Amant. It is true that in Théophile's poem, if action is not directly described, it is constantly implied. The resolution of the poem takes place in
terms of the gradual isolation of the lovers. But the actions
are most important in reflecting attitudes, and narrative interest is certainly not in control of the poem. Saint-Amant's
poem, on the other hand, has no real plot, no real complexity
or evolution: it is a simple meditative poem cast in the form
almost of an epistle. At the same time it has certain of the
more elementary features of Théophile's poem, and could
be profitably compared in its Baroque characteristics to it

and to other French poems of the time, notably Tristan l'Hermite's "Promenoir des deux amants." [5]

In contrast to Théophile's poem, the poems of Donne to be considered next resolve themselves less in terms of action than of emotions. Since action, implied or described, is reduced to a minimum, the evolution of attitudes in the speaker and audience (and eventually in the reader) can more swiftly and more concentratedly become complex. Théophile's poem and the poems of Donne may be thus contrasted, not of course absolutely but in some degree. Donne's poems are shorter and the attitudes more complex. Their success may be thought of as a technical advance over the poems whose rhetorical situations we have already considered. With the possible exception of Milton's "Lycidas," they probably achieve the greatest rhetorical complexity of any poems written in the Baroque age. And the degree of skill whereby they reach that complexity is certainly one of the highest points attained by the Baroque tendency toward what we have called dramaticality.

5. See Imbrie Buffum's explication of Saint-Amant's "La Solitude" in his *Studies in the Baroque from Montaigne to Rotrou*, pp. 140–48.

10. Poems of Donne

Looking at Donne's *Songs and Sonets* as a whole, we see that they offer a wide range of rhetorical situations. There are poems, like "The Good-morrow," "The Flea," "The Prohibition," "A Lecture upon the Shadow," which are addressed directly to the beloved. The rhetorical structure is simple enough; in fact, whatever complexity those poems have derives from other sources than the rhetorical situation. Even simpler are the poems in which audience and reader are merged, as in the "Song: Goe, and catche a falling starre" and "Negative Love." The latter may not be a pure example. But certainly in the former there is no distinction between audience and reader. It is nonetheless a brilliant exercise in a narrow rhetorical situation. The reader-audience is not merely addressed, he is put to work; in effect, he is sent on a fantastic and fruitless journey to prove the speaker's point. Most of the *Songs and Sonets*, however, have their full complement of rhetorical members. It is chiefly from these poems that I shall pick examples, to show Donne's skill in developing rhetorical structure and thus to suggest a way in which his achievement may be brought into a general scheme of European Baroque style in poetry.

I shall consider, first of all, two examples of Donne's poetry in which there is a single audience. Then I shall go on to consider two poems in which the audience is multiple. Within each type the first poem will be relatively simple, and the second relatively complex. As before, the poems will be considered not as static objects but as performances, existing and unfolding in time. It is appropriate in this regard to mention Leonard Unger's essay on Donne's poetry and to say that his attempt to define the style of Donne succeeds insofar as it rejects the notion of extended metaphor as a total characterization and insofar as it substitutes complexity of attitudes.[1] But, perhaps for polemical reasons, Unger is less concerned with how the complexity of attitudes evolves than with the fact of its existence. One major source of complexity, as I shall try to show, is the evolution of attitudes within the poem.

As a poem having a relatively simple rhetorical situation with a single explicit audience, let us consider "Loves Growth."[2] From the start we are aware of a speaker in the first person:

> I Scarce beleeve my love to be so pure
>   As I had thought it was,
>   Because it doth endure
> Vicissitude, and season, as the grasse;
> Me thinks I lyed all winter, when I swore,
> My love was infinite, if spring make'it more.

1. *Donne's Poetry and Modern Criticism* (Chicago, 1950), now reprinted in *The Man in the Name*, Minneapolis, 1956.

2. See below, pp. 231–32. All the texts of Donne are from H. J. C. Grierson's edition, *The Poems of John Donne*, Oxford, 1912. The first collected edition of Donne's poetry did not appear until 1633, two years after his death. But most of his *Songs and Sonets* must have been written in the 1590's and in the first decade of the 1600's, according to the testimony of Ben Jonson, and other evidence. The poems I discuss have, of course, been explicated many times and in many ways.

But in what does the audience consist? For the time being
we have to content ourselves with a provisional audience:
the reader finds himself in a double role as reader and audience both. The second stanza carries on in the same tone.
Love is not transcendent ("infinite" or "pure" or "abstract"),
but contingent and mutable ("mixt of all stuffes"). Thus
love, which seemed perfect and infinite, is actually suscepti-
ble to change and growth. How is it possible to resolve the
difficulty? It is possible to do so, as the speaker does, by
thinking of love becoming not larger but more "eminent,"
just as the sun does not "enlarge" but rather "shows" the
stars.[3] So, by a concatenation of four metaphors the speaker
reinforces his solution to the problem: first the relation of
sun to stars, then love blossoming from a bough, concentric
circles in "water stir'd," and finally concentric spheres. They
are metaphors of many in one, variety in unity; and it is
the speaker's purpose to characterize in those terms his new-
found complex view of love. Once the difficulty has been
coped with, the speaker can safely narrow his audience
down to the particular beloved:

> Those like so many spheares, but one heaven make,
> For, they are all concentrique unto thee.

It might be argued that the specific second-person audience
("thee") was implied even before, in the fifth line from
the end, it is explicitly mentioned. But if we are to read the
poem as performance, we must take what is given us when
it is given. We must always be asking ourselves, why does
the poet say such-and-such a thing now and not later?[4] In

3. Grierson's note (Vol. 2, p. 31) makes it clear, without tracing the
astronomical doctrine, that the verb "showne" in the text means something
like "enhanced."

4. It is a further question whether introducing the second-person audience
toward the end of a poem is not a common Renaissance practice. One would
have to say that it is. But in most instances such poems in the Renaissance

time, then, the speaker's attitude does evolve. He solves his difficulty concerning the nature of his love. And in the process he evolves a new attitude toward his beloved. The most obvious sign of this evolution of attitude is the fact that he refrains from addressing his audience directly until almost the end of the poem.

A still more radical evolution of attitude is to be found in "The Sunne Rising" (below, pages 233–34). As in the previous poem, the audience is single, not multiple. But in contrast to "Loves Growth," the audience is from the start quite specific: "Busie old foole, unruly Sunne," the poem begins, and the speaker's words continue throughout to be addressed to the sun. The speaker refers to himself (for the first time in the second stanza) in the first person; but just as often he speaks in the first person plural, thus referring, as the reader soon discovers, to himself and his beloved. This almost casual alternation between "I" and "we" enhances the fact, important for the poem, that the lovers together make up a kind of microcosmos. We may, then, assume that the beloved acquiesces in what the speaker says, and remains a passive or merely coordinate agent in the poem.

If we look at the opening and conclusion, we see at once that in order to succeed, the poem must undergo a radical evolution of attitudes. At the beginning the speaker's tone is querulous, almost belligerent:

> Busie old foole, unruly Sunne,
>   Why dost thou thus,
> Through windowes, and through curtaines call on us?
> Must to thy motions lovers seasons run?
>   Sawcy pedantique wretch, goe chide.
>   Late schoole boyes, and sowre prentices . . .

-----

actually end with the direct address, which serves the same purpose as the *envoi* of a ballade (see Shakespeare's *Sonnets*, e.g., numbers 30, 62, 107, etc.). In Donne's poem, however, the second-person audience is just below the surface from the start. It rises finally in line 24, only to submerge again.

Nevertheless, by the end of the poem the speaker's tone has become almost gentle and ingratiating:

> Thou sunne art halfe as happy'as wee,
> In that the world's contracted thus;
> Thine age askes ease, and since thy duties bee
> To warme the world, that's done in warming us.
> Shine here to us, and thou art every where;
> This bed thy center is, these walls, thy spheare.

At first the sun is uncontrollable and therefore intrusively irritating; but somehow its powers are at last curtailed to such an extent that the speaker's attitude becomes almost patronizing if not pitying. How is it that so radical a change can take place in a unified poem? Does the speaker's attitude evolve or does it merely shift? To answer these questions, to understand the rhetorical structure of the poem, let us follow the text line by line and in effect perform it in time.

In the first stanza the speaker, indignant at the sun's intrusion, tries to dismiss it:

> Sawcy pedantique wretch, goe chide
> Late schoole boyes, and sowre prentices,
> Goe tell Court-huntsmen, that the King will ride,
> Call countrey ants to harvest offices . . .

Love, he argues, does not depend on time; it is, by implication, eternal. The initial paradox, then, is that love, which is eternal, is represented or embodied in two mortal lovers: the sun, representing time, *should* have nothing to do with love (in the form of the two lovers), yet it nevertheless intrudes. It is the force of that blunt paradox that provokes the speaker's anger. In the second stanza, as a kind of insolent strategy, the speaker minimizes the power of the sun. By the mere fact that he can blink his eyes he argues that he has the power to eclipse the sun, and yet he refrains from doing so in order not to lose for even a few moments the sight of his beloved:

> Thy beames, so reverend, and strong
> Why shouldst thou thinke?
> I could eclipse and cloud them with a winke,
> But that I would not lose her sight so long . . .

The speaker even urges the sun to go about its trivial course, just to see that it can discover in the real world nothing the lovers do not contain. And while the sun is running his useless course witnesses will watch the lovers and will be able to report that everything the sun saw took place between the lovers:

> If her eyes have not blinded thine,
> Looke, and to morrow late, tell mee,
> Whether both the'India's of spice and Myne
> Be where thou leftst them, or lie here with mee.
> Ask for those Kings whom thou saw'st yesterday,
> And thou shalt heare, All here in one bed lay.

In the course of two stanzas the speaker's attitude of rude dismissal has gradually given way to one of conciliatory explanation. It is as if the speaker realizes that the blunt paradox of the beginning must be softened. He therefore faces the paradox, and in doing so modifies his attitude toward the sun. We cannot say that the speaker's shifts are sudden. In effect, the second stanza presents us with a riddle; and in the process of presenting the riddle or arguing his case, the speaker gradually adopts a gentler tone. Though the reader may in the second stanza have come to suspect the answer to the riddle, his suspicions are fully confirmed only at the beginning of the third:

> She'is all States, and all Princes, I,
> Nothing else is.

At this point the speaker's explanation becomes clear and his attitude toward the sun becomes almost solicitous. For the paradox has finally been explored and established: the lovers themselves are a cosmos, albeit a microcosmos, and consequently contain *in parvo* every part of the real world, the macrocosmos. The converse must also be true, as the speaker asserts, that anything not contained in the microcosmos does not exist in the macrocosmos. For the purposes of the poem we must accept the notion, just as, for instance, in Marvell's "The Garden" we must accept the belief that all things on land have their correspondences in the sea. In accepting that notion we come to see how the poem establishes and rationalizes the blunt paradox at the beginning. In the present context it is most important to note how the speaker, in the process of explaining and confirming the paradox, changes his attitude toward the sun. At first, to recapitulate, he is hostile toward it. The poem bursts forth in two belligerent questions. It continues in a series of contemptuous imperatives. And the first stanza ends in a haughty assertion. The second stanza also begins with a question, this time more poised, with the effect of disparaging the sun's exalted position. Then comes an assertion; and the stanza concludes with a series of gently provocative imperatives. All of the third and last stanza, except for the final two lines, is cast in the assertive mode, giving a tone of mastery and assurance to the speaker's words:

> She'is all States, and all Princes, I,
>   Nothing else is.
> Princes doe but play us; compar'd to this,
> All honor's mimique; All wealth alchimie.
>   Thou sunne art halfe as happy'as wee,
>   In that the world's contracted thus;
>   Thine age askes ease, and since thy duties bee
>   To warme the world, that's done in warming us.

The tables are turned. Instead of berating the sun for its intrusion upon the lovers, the speaker invites it to shine upon them even at the expense of the macrocosmos. There can then be no conflict between the sun (representing time) and the lovers (representing eternal love), for the lovers, as well as love, are not only eternal but universal:

> This bed thy center is, these walls, thy spheare.
> Shine here to us, and thou art every where.

In these last lines the speaker all but loses the explanatory, patronizing attitude which succeeded his first impatient attitude toward the sun, and becomes expansively cordial and almost pityingly solicitous; in effect, he orients the sun in what should be its proper function and invites it to make itself at home.

We have witnessed step by step a most remarkable change in attitude. Within an unbroken rhetorical situation, the relation between the several members has evolved from one extreme to another—from, in barest terms, hostility to solicitousness. Watching the change take place, we have discovered the stable paradox which underlies the poem. It, too, in a sense is evolved; for it is first stated bluntly and uncompromisingly and is then modified and explained so that it becomes (if one accepts at least poetically the supporting doctrine) reasonable and conclusive. The mainspring of the poem's rhetorical structure is, obviously, the relationship between speaker and audience. Though the reader's role is implicit throughout, it is not of the same importance. Much of the speaker's argumentation, however, is directed as much to the reader as to the audience. The reader's function is to follow the course of argument, to take first the side of the speaker and then that of the sun, and finally to own that the sun has been, by implication, totally mastered. Even the sun's role *seems* to change. As a matter of fact, the poet does not insist upon its changing, since, of course, that would violate excessively the reader's sense of propriety. But in effect, as the speaker becomes reconciled through his own arguments to the sun's presence, the sun itself seems to change from an insolent intruder to a docile servant in the power of its master.

All the three modes of discourse are employed to advantage, if we consider imperatives as exclamations. Particularly the use of questions and imperatives creates the effect of the passage of time from moment to moment. That effect of momentaneousness, together with the constantly active presence of the speaker, emphasizes the aspect of the poem as performance. As the poem progresses, the effect of localization becomes more pronounced: "lie *here* with mee" (line 18), "All *here* in one bed" (20), "compar'd to *this*" (23), "In that the world's contracted *thus*" (26), "Shine *here* to us" (29), "*This* bed thy center is, *these* walls, thy spheare" (30). By means of such repetition the relationships between the various rhetorical members become more precise. In a meaningful sense the opposite is taken into account: the conclusion of the poem is not simple but complex. In fact, the opposite, that the sun *is* an intruder or that its real function *is* to revolve around the macrocosmos, is faced at the very beginning. It is from this point that the poem moves toward its stable paradox.

In contrast to "Loves Growth," "The Sunne Rising" develops a complex rhetorical situation which arises step by step from the gradually changing relationships between the rhetorical members. In "Loves Growth" the evolution of attitudes is much less clear, since the second-person audience enters explicitly only late in the poem and, compared to the sun, does not take a very active part in developing the rhetorical situation. The contrast between the two poems is not absolute, however. In fact, they both proceed according to the same logic. The one begins with the blunt paradox that love, which is infinite, seems to grow, the other with the blunt paradox that love, though independent of time, seems endangered by the sun. Both paradoxes are stabilized in the end; but in the one poem the process is much less in terms of the rhetorical situation than in the other. "The Sunne Rising," in achieving its complex dramatic effect, makes use of a number of enhancing devices, such as questions, exclamations, localization, and including the opposite. On the other hand, "Loves Growth" is all assertion; it makes almost no attempt at localization; and it talks more about taking the opposite into account than actually doing so. All the same, both poems, the one with restricted means, the other with great resources, manage to evolve a set of attitudes in terms of a rhetorical situation.

To find a simple example of a poem having a multiple audience, it is necessary to go outside the *Songs and Sonets;* since within that collection there seems to be only one example of a poem with multiple audience, "Twicknam Garden," and it is rather complex. First, therefore, I shall consider "Elegie XII: His Parting from Her" (see below, pages 235–38), a poem which is closer to the Renaissance practice of catalogue audiences, and then proceed to discuss the virtuoso performance of "Twicknam Garden."

In the "Elegie" the speaker of the poem moves through a change in attitude which begins in despair and ends in constancy and affirmation. He does so in terms of four successive audiences: Night, Love, Fortune, and the Beloved ("dearest Friend"). The poem begins with an invocation to Night as, among other things, the symbol of despair:

> Since she must go, and I must mourn, come Night,
> Environ me with darkness, whilst I write.

But Night cannot dispel the fires of Love. And in line 13 the audience changes and Love is directly interrogated:

> Oh Love, that fire and darkness should be mixt,
> Or to thy Triumphs soe strange torments fixt?
> Is't because thou thy self art blind, that wee
> Thy Martyrs must no more each other see?
> Or tak'st thou pride to break us on the wheel,

And view old Chaos in the Pains we feel?
Or have we left undone some mutual Right,
Through holy fear, that merits thy despight?

It is not Love in only one of his aspects; he is both tormentor
and life-giver, both feared and desired. And yet Love is not
to be blamed for his double nature. At first the speaker takes
the guilt upon himself, but then imputes it to Love's blind-
ness. He proceeds, however, to recount his and his mistress'
devotion to the duties of Love; and concludes that it cannot be Love but rather Fortune that makes the lovers part.
It is therefore with new confidence that the speaker addresses Fortune. He has found the true enemy:

Oh Fortune, thou'rt not worth my least exclame,
And plague enough thou hast in thy own shame.
Do thy great worst, my friend and I have armes,
Though not against thy strokes, against thy harmes.

In the process the speaker "discovers" that Love (always half
personified) does not depend upon presence or absence. As he
says to Fortune,

Rend us in sunder, thou canst not divide
Our bodies so, but that our souls are ty'd,
And we can love by letters still and gifts,
And thoughts and dreams; Love never wanteth shifts.

So far the speaker has evolved an attitude which began in
despair and went through several stages of doubt concerning
the nature of true love. In terms of audiences, the speaker's
attitude toward Night was favorable. He desired the protection of darkness. But since Love's fires still burned, that was
only apparent protection. The speaker's attitude continued
to develop in terms of Love in his double aspect. In the end
the speaker absolved Love, as well as himself and his Beloved,
from the crime of inconstancy.

The speaker's attack on Fortune, the real enemy, consolidates his own position: his love does not depend on time and space, Fortune's dimensions. When the speaker finally turns to address his last audience, the Beloved, he is secure enough in his new attitude to join her in spurning two previous audiences, Night and Fortune. The other audience, Love, is found to be not only guiltless, but desirable. Thus the speaker's attitude has evolved so far that he is able to look upon Night and Fortune with equanimity, to counsel his Beloved against despair and inconstancy, and finally to declare his own unchanging love:

> Take therefore all in this: I love so true,
> As I will never look for less in you.

So it is that the speaker begins in despair and doubt and ends in constancy and certitude. The change in attitude is, as we have seen, gradual. And it occurs in terms of the four audiences. In fact, the speaker's attitude toward the first three audiences is made even more explicit than usual in such poems, because each of the audiences is not only addressed but talked about, and either praised or blamed. In other words, the speaker has not only a second person, but also a third person attitude toward them.

As means of making the situation dramatic, the poem uses questions and exclamations (usually vocative). But there is almost no attempt at localization, nor are the various rhetorical members characterized vividly in terms of action. One might say that the evolution of the speaker's attitude comes about all too gradually, and that it does not sufficiently imply changes of attitude on the part of the rhetorical members. The next poem to be considered is more successful in working out its rhetorical situation.

Returning to the *Songs and Sonets*, let us look at "Twicknam Garden" as a more complex example of a poem with multiple audience (see below, pages 239–40). In it a transformation takes place: the lover, speaker of the poem, becomes a fountain. At the same time, a change takes place in the speaker's attitude. And both transformation and change are reflected in the succession of four audiences the speaker addresses. The first audience is, in effect, the speaker himself:

> Blasted with sighs, and surrounded with teares,
> > Hither I come to seeke the spring,
> > And at mine eyes, and at mine eares,
> Receive such balmes, as else cure every thing;
> > But O, selfe traytor, I do bring
> The spider love, which transubstantiates all,
> > And can convert Manna to gall,
> And that this place may thoroughly be thought
> > True Paradise, I have the serpent brought.

It could be argued that the phrase "selfe traytor" is apposi- tive and not vocative, that the speaker is only describing and not addressing himself. But it is perhaps best to leave the phrase ambiguous; it at least suggests that the speaker takes himself for his audience. In the first stanza, then, his nature is split. On the one hand, he desires relief from his painful love; in this role he is mild and beseeching. But on the other hand, he cannot bring himself to give up his love; and in this role he is sardonic almost to the point of flippancy. In terms of the first audience, therefore, the speaker exhibits a kind of wry self-pity.

In the second stanza the audience changes, as the speaker turns from himself to address Love:

> 'Twere wholsomer for mee, that winter did
> > Benight the glory of this place,
> > And that a grave frost did forbid
> These trees to laugh, and mocke mee to my face;
> > But that I may not this disgrace
> Indure, nor yet leave loving, Love let mee
> > Some senslesse peece of this place bee;

> Make me a mandrake, so I may groane here,
>   Or a stone fountaine weeping out my yeare.[5]

Addressing a new audience has the effect of amalgamating
the two sides of the speaker. By implication, he is becoming
resigned to the paradoxical position of desiring relief and
keeping his love. It would be better for me in my ridiculous
position, he suggests, if the garden were in the grip of a frost.
But that is no real solution. He therefore appeals to Love to
make him a part of the garden, a mandrake or a fountain. It
is not a groveling appeal, for the speaker maintains his almost
flippant attitude by suggesting casually either one or the
other transformation. In his new double role he still tries to
give an impression of insouciance.

The resolution of the speaker's predicament comes as he
assumes himself transformed into a fountain: he is neither
cured of his love nor made to suffer for it in human form;
also, in a sense, he has made his love public:

> Hither with christall vyals, lovers come,
>   And take my teares, which are loves wine,
>   And try your mistresse Teares at home,
> For all are false, that tast not just like mine;
>   Alas, hearts do not in eyes shine,
> Nor can you more judge womans thoughts by teares,
>   Than by her shadow, what she weares.

The audience has changed from Love to lovers in general;
from a more or less private to a public audience. Correspond-
ingly, the speaker's attitude has changed from that of a sardonic self-centered lover to that of a cynical but exhibitionist
exemplar. From his new position the speaker can face his

5. Some editors prefer the reading "nor leave this garden" for "nor yet
leave loving." The alternate reading has the support of several manuscripts
("none of very high textual authority," according to Grierson, Vol. 2, p. 26)
and the editions from 1635 to 1669. Poetically the second reading is probably
preferable. But since it is not a crucial point in my analysis, I shall not take
the time to defend or attack either choice.

suffering publicly. With new-found strength, therefore, he confronts his fourth and last audience:

> O perverse sexe, where none is true but shee,
> Who's therefore true, because her truth kills me.

The attack is directed against the Beloved, of course; but in his new public role the speaker finds himself talking in terms of the whole of womankind. It is significant that the speaker refrains from alluding to the Beloved until the very end, after his own suffering has gradually been made public. The whole evolution of attitude is carried out in terms of the various audiences addressed throughout the poem. In the process the original paradox, the lover wishing to be cured and yet not lose his love, gives way to a stabler paradox, the lover insisting on the truth of his tears and yet complaining that his Beloved remains true—that is, chaste and unyielding.

Again, the reader's role is that of chief witness. He must follow one by one the actions the speaker describes himself doing. He must hear the speaker address the several audiences. Though rather passive in the role assigned him, the reader has a very important function in underlying the changes in audience; that he is a source of unity for the poem is stressed in the last two lines ("O perverse sexe . . ."), which are ambiguously addressed either to womankind or to the reader,[6] and probably to both. Another means whereby the speaker and reader are more closely related is the rather intense effect of localization achieved through the repetition of locative adverbs and demonstrative adjectives. Though the speaker is egocentric, his suffering is in terms of the garden, in terms increasingly public: "Hither" (line 1), "this place" (8, 11), "These trees" (13), "this place" (16), "here" (17), "Hither" (19). Both the intense localization and the express

---

6. "O perverse sexe . . ." may either be vocative in the second person or exclamatory in the third. In the first alternative the lines are directed to womankind; in the second, to the reader. The first is probably the dominant alternative.

desire to become part of the garden (lines 14–18) prepare the speaker for his public role, and thus relate him more closely to the reader.

Despite the fact that the speaker sees his plight in increasingly public terms, it might be urged that his arguments continue to be irrationally self-interested. But there is no necessary contradiction, especially since the lover is a fictional character and argues quite appropriately by lover's logic. There seems, then, to be a clear evolution in the speaker's attitude. The succession of audiences, from self to Love to lovers, bolsters the change; so that in the end the speaker is able, by his own reasoning, to spend his public wrath, however indirectly, on his Beloved, and in doing so pay her a rueful compliment. All the same, the evolution of attitude is not radical, since throughout the poem the speaker retains a basic egocentric self-pity. Even if the speaker's position is logically untenable or perhaps morally repugnant, it is nevertheless dramatically justified. And in dramatic terms the poem, seen as a gradual characterization of the speaker, does evolve. Its stable paradox is the speaker's rationalization, which does not stand by itself but rather serves to characterize the speaker.

It would be worth while to consider the four poems of Donne just analyzed purely as examples of technical achievement. In part that is what I have tried to do. It is also worth while to go further and attempt generalizations in terms of literary history. Donne is one of the first to make use of the rhetorical situation in the lyric in such a way as to present a complex change, an evolution, in the speaker's attitude. One could go on and include, giving proper evidence, many poems of Vaughan, Milton, and Marvell, to name three other major poets of the age. Certainly, in any characterization of Baroque style, their highly developed use of the rhetorical situation must be taken into account. It can also be related to the growing tendency toward dramaticality. Previously, in the Renaissance lyric, there were certainly dramatic elements:

questions, quoted conversation, emphatic repetitions. One may think of Wyatt or Ronsard, or go back as far as Petrarch. But among other things, what distinguishes their poems from the major achievements of the Baroque age is the lack of attention to time and evolution of attitude. As a final exercise, to make conclusions more secure, I shall take up again Milton's "Lycidas" and consider it now from the point of view of its rhetorical situation.

11. Milton's "Lycidas" Again

Since all elements of style are in some way interrelated, different approaches to a poem can lead ultimately to the same discovery. We have already seen that "Lycidas" [1] has a complex time structure which is a major part of the main structure of the poem. Another major part is the rhetorical structure, already touched upon but worthy of fuller exploration. The trend we have followed in Baroque poetry toward greater dramaticality is well represented in "Lycidas." The poem is emphatically a poem as performance: most of the rhetorical devices I have singled out for special stress are used, and the full rhetorical situation is exploited. My purpose now will be to show, in several important ways, how the poem "works" as a rhetorical structure.

It is convenient to think of "Lycidas" as divided into three main sections: lines 1–84, 85–164, and 165–85. This is not a rigid division, but it will provide bearings for a discussion of the rhetorical movement. In the first part the whole rhetorical situation is firmly established. Speaker, reader, and several audiences are characterized, and, in particular, the

1. For the text, see below, pp. 214–19.

speaker's attitude is to a certain point evolved. From the start a direct relationship is formed between the speaker and the first audience. For the speaker, in the character of poet-mourner, speaks in the first person to his audience, the honorific plants (laurels, myrtles, and ivy), which are addressed in the vocative. By means of this first audience a great deal is accomplished. Not only is the importance of the occasion, the death of a poet, established, but also to some extent the duty, if not the fitness, of the speaker to assume the role of mourner. "Who would sing for Lycidas?": someone must undertake the charge, even an inexperienced poet "with forc'd fingers rude." Since not much can be accomplished dramatically with an audience as unresponsive as plants, without running the danger of excessive personification, the speaker then turns to a new audience, the Muses, endowed by convention with greater animation and personality than plants. As if to embolden himself he urges them on: "Hence with denial vain, and coy excuse." And quite appropriately he proceeds to lay some small claim to honor as a poet:

> So may some gentle Muse
> With lucky words favour my destin'd Urn,
> And as he passes turn,
> And bid fair peace to be my sable shroud.

The passage also serves as a kind of transition. It is not strictly addressed to the Muses. In fact, in this first part of the poem, the tendency is to move away from the particular audience, plants or Muses, and address a general audience which is in effect the reader. As the speaker goes on to describe his past friendship with Lycidas, strengthening his claim as poet-mourner, the poem moves out of touch with any particular audience. Gradually the reader assumes the responsibility of judging the speaker's fitness. Up to this point, then, the speaker has proceeded in terms of two audiences (the second more animate than the first) and the reader. He has presented his credentials. And his attitude has developed from a sense of sad duty to a sense of the degree of his loss measured in terms of past joy.

When the speaker turns to address Lycidas directly for the first time, his attitude veers, naturally enough, to despair:

> But O the heavy change, now thou art gone,
> Now thou art gone, and never must return!

The speaker does not allow his grief to become sentimental or purely personal; loss of Lycidas is expressed in terms of Nature, as having the effect of canker, taint-worm, or frost. Thus the poem makes a transition to the third audience (not counting the reader or Lycidas), which is the benign presences of Nature in the form of nymphs. They are chided ("Where were ye Nymphs") but then absolved of any guilt:

> Ay me, I fondly dream!
> Had ye been there—for what could that have done?

On the speaker's part it is a wild attempt to assuage his sorrow by fixing upon someone or something the responsibility for Lycidas' death—an attempt which the speaker himself checks because it is groundless and can serve no purpose. Dramatically it is highly effective. As the speaker's attitude evolves from sorrow to despair, the three audiences (again not counting the reader or Lycidas) succeed one upon the other with an effect of growing intensity. The plants were least involved in the death of Lycidas; the speaker had almost to apologize for disturbing them. It was easier to approach the Muses, once it had been established that Lycidas was a poet and therefore, generically within their range of concern. But even they had to be urged on. Merely in point of suggested movement, the plants and the Muses are stationary and somewhat passive. The Nymphs, however, are a degree higher in animation. They can wander where they like, and so their responsibility is potentially greater. Their concern is also greater, since they knew Lycidas himself as a person; he was their "loved Lycidas." Hence the speaker's attitude evolves in terms of a series of audiences, each one more concerned with the death of Lycidas, first as worthy man, then as poet, and then as particular person. At the point of most intense grief, in the midst of reckless accusation, the speaker breaks off and, absolving the Nymphs (and with them, to some extent, pagan Nature), turns to address the reader in objective terms on the ultimate question of existence. In the whole passage on heavenly reward, the speaker is working out his despair in purely pagan terms. He has already suggested that pagan Nature is not hostile to worth and virtue, a doctrine which resounds through the ancient moralists from Plato to Cicero. And he goes on to this consolation from the pagan view of heaven, which, though it does not guarantee immortality, at least promises the due reward of immortal fame. The speaker's attitude, then, has reached a sort of equilibrium. His grief remains, but it is tempered by the benevolence of Nature and the possibility of *some* heavenly reward.

Thus, as the first part of the poem ends, speaker and reader are prepared for a calmer, more formal and public mourning. The second part, which begins and ends with an apostrophe to personified Nature, contains the procession of mourners, Triton, Camus, and Peter. But in a sense we may consider Nature herself as a mourner in the changing form of Arethuse; Mincius; Alpheus; the "Sicilian Muse" (that is, the Muse of bucolic poetry); and finally the flowered valleys. All, except the rustic Muse, are presences of Nature, and perhaps the Muse should be made no exception. Rhetorically speaking, this second part has no one clearly defined audience. Nature, under several guises, presides at the beginning and end and may be said to remain throughout the procession of mourners as a kind of witness. She is invoked in one of her forms at the beginning:

> O Fountain Arethuse, and thou honour'd flood
> Smooth-sliding Mincius, crown'd with vocal reeds,
> That strain I heard was of a higher mood:

> But now my Oat proceeds,
> And listens to the Herald of the Sea
> That came in Neptune's plea.[2]

But as the passage continues, the audience is left in suspension: not entirely disposed of and yet not reinforced. To some extent the reader takes over. He has served as judge of the speaker's qualifications and witness of his despair and, in pagan terms, affirmation. He becomes now a spectator of the mournful pageant. The rhetorical situation, then, does not break down. Nature, though for a while in the background, remains the audience; and during the procession itself the reader comes to the fore as a kind of spectator. As for the speaker, he arranges and sponsors the procession. How his attitude changes must be inferred from the choice and order of the mourners. For he does not comment upon their statements but rather, first in indirect discourse and then in direct quotation, presents them.

The first mourner, Triton ("Herald of the Sea"), serves to absolve Nature from any guilt, continuing the theme of Nature's benevolence already struck in terms of the Nymphs: the efficient cause of Lycidas' death rests with the "fatal and perfidious Bark / Built in th'eclipse and rigg'd with curses dark." Nature is represented also in the next mourner; but Camus, in contrast to Triton, is directly, personally, concerned with the death of Lycidas. The first mourner is interested in defending Nature from the charge of guilt, and thus represents objective Nature; the second represents mourning Nature, and thus resumes the same theme established earlier (lines 37–49).

Up to this point, considering all that has gone before, Lycidas has been mourned as a personal loss by the speaker (chiefly lines 23–49), implicitly by the Nymphs, and briefly by Camus. The third mourner, Peter, carries the grief into a public or

2. As well as being representatives of Nature, the fountain and river are literary allusions to Theocritus and Virgil.

even a social dimension. His is a rational weighing of the loss, the extent of which is expressed in terms of contrast: there are too many greedy and negligent shepherds to allow society to take Lycidas' death lightly. Besides the speaker's grief, this is the first expression of human mourning; thematically it points ahead to the third part of the poem. To speak of Peter as human is not doing violence to the poem or to what everybody knows—that he is a saint. In order to avoid breaking the predominantly pagan tendency of the first two parts of the poem, the poet abstains from actually naming Peter; rather, he refers to him as "The Pilot of the Galilean lake." Certainly, the Christian associations are there ("Galilean," the keys, "his Mitred locks," the sheepherding metaphor which alludes to John 10:1–18), but they are not yet related to Christian doctrine. It serves the poet's purpose to conceal as much as possible. Peter does not even mention Christian salvation, though ordinarily one would expect him, chief of Christ's Disciples, to do so. In fact, the concealment is so successful—mostly because the sheepherding fiction is common to both pagan and Christian tradition—that whatever Christian overtones are heard may be stored up as presages of the final Christian resolution of the poem.

Peter's appearance, therefore, cannot be said to break the pagan tendency. What it accomplishes is the realization of the whole trend of the second part: the formal, public nature of the procession that was begun as a kind of inquest and continued as an expression of personal grief is finally corroborated in the figure of Peter, whose words go beyond assigning guilt and voicing personal sorrow to surveying the loss in social terms. Since it provides all concerned with the possibility of clear-eyed consolation, Peter's speech does not make a violent contrast with the following regretful, almost wistful passage on flowers to decorate the "Laureate Hearse." That there is some contrast can hardly be denied; for when Peter finishes, the speaker again addresses Nature ("Return Alpheus, the dread voice is past, / That shrunk thy streams . . ."), calling attention to the change in tone. But the statement also calls attention to the continuity preserved throughout the second part: Nature's rather timid presence as audience is re-emphasized, and the procession is skillfully set off from the rest of the passage.

Presumably the speaker's attitude has been further modified by the procession. It had evolved from despair to a kind of pagan hope; it existed in terms of the speaker himself and of Nature. Now that the mourning has been made formal and social, the speaker is able to continue and perform the obsequies which, according to custom, are due the dead. There is some consolation merely in going through the conventional formalities. In the act of commemoration the speaker links himself with Nature, whose flowers he asks for. He also links himself with a kind of vague public:

> For so to interpose a little ease,
> Let our frail thoughts dally with false surmise.

The plural "our" is significant. Before, the speaker kept himself separate from other mourners, but now—chiefly, one must say, as a result of the procession—he considers himself not alone among the human, or at least the personal, mourners. And throughout the rest of the poem the speaker never refers to himself again as alone, but more and more identifies himself with others.[3] The lines lead on in another way. They recognize how shallow the customary obsequies are, since there is not even a hearse to adorn. In pagan terms it is a horrible thing that the body should go unburied.[4] That is

3. The exclamation "Ay me!" in line 154 need not invalidate the statement.

4. For a suggestive parallel to Lycidas' plight, see Virgil's account of Aeneas' meeting with Palinurus in *Aeneid* 6. Palinurus asks Aeneas either to take him across Acheron somehow or throw earth upon his body ("tu mihi terram / inice"). The Sibyl speaks to him as "inhumatus" and holds out to him "duri solacia casus": his bones will be appeased "aeternumque locus Palinuri nomen habebit." Moreover, the parallel leads us on further to the covert presence of Arion and Melicertes in the address to the Dolphins.

the final, most inexorable grounds for despair. Only now has the speaker's attitude evolved to the point where it can bear to face the heaviest grief of all. And with a kind of calm resolution or controlled despair the speaker dwells upon the fate of Lycidas' unburied body:

> . . . Whilst thee the shores, and sounding Seas
> Wash far away, where'er thy bones are hurl'd . . .

The passage (lines 154–62) is directly addressed to Lycidas, whose body retains a kind of shadow identity: he is "visiting" or "sleeping." And yet it is obviously just the speaker's imagination that endows the body with any animation. To some extent it is a version of the pagan notion that the spirit of an unburied body will wander until the body is found and buried. Here, however, the "unlaid" spirit is identified with the weltering body; for the separation of spirit and body is being saved for the Christian affirmation of the third and last part of the poem.

Just before the third part there are again foreshadowings of the final Christian resolution. After a reference to St. Michael's Mount in Cornwall,

> Where the great vision of the guarded Mount
> Looks toward Namancos and Bayona's hold,

the speaker calls upon the "Angel," as if Michael were standing on the promontory, to "Look homeward" (presumably north to the Irish Sea [5]), thus introducing a minor audience, through which he suggests, however vaguely, the possibility of supernatural compassion or even intercession. Again in the next line the audience changes:

> And O ye Dolphins, waft the hapless youth.

5. On another level the Angel is asked to "Look Homeward" to an England beset with religious and political dissension. Before the Angel guarded England against Spain; now the danger is at home.

There is a definite progression in the two audiences. Michael (if by "Angel" Michael is meant [6]) suggests the Judaic tradition, which does not necessarily admit immortality. The Archangel is called upon only to sympathize. On the other hand, the Dolphins have a more active role. They are called upon to "waft"—that is, "to convey safely by water" [7]—the body of Lycidas. Not only do the Dolphins have a more active role, they also have a range of resonance which supplements and transcends the function of the Archangel Michael. In Antiquity dolphins were known as friendly and even sacred animals; they were almost tutelary spirits of the ocean. [8] It is especially appropriate that dolphins should be invoked for Lycidas, since they were thought in Antiquity to be most helpful to poets: witness the widespread legends of Arion and Melicertes, both poets rescued by dolphins. [9] There was also a cult of Apollo Delphinios, which suggests even closer connections. Moreover, in Christian tradition the dolphin has often appeared as a symbol of the Christian and sometimes, especially with an anchor as the Cross, as a symbol of Christ. [10] In the space of two lines, then, the speaker suggests

6. "If," in M. Y. Hughes' words, "the thought in lines 161–2 is parenthetical, the *Angel* is Lycidas; but the play on *Looks—Look* suggests that Michael is meant" (see his edition, p. 295). Professor Hughes' conclusion seems valid. There is no good reason why Lycidas should be called an angel.

7. See Hughes' note, p. 295, and the *NED, S.* "Waft," 2.

8. According to Pauly-Wissowa, "die Sage weiss zu erzahlen, dass sie [dolphins] Menschen retten und Leichen ans Land tragen, damit sie der Bestattung teilhaftig werden . . ." *Real-Encyklopadie der klassischen Altertumswissenschaft* (Stuttgart, 1901), *4*, cols. 2504–09.

9. For Arion see Herodotus, 1.23–24; for Melicertes, Pausanias, 1.44, 7–8, 2.1, 3.

10. "The particular idea is that of swiftness and celerity symbolizing the desire with which Christians, who are thus represented as being sharers in the nature of Christ the true Fish, should seek after the knowledge of Christ." "Speaking generally, the dolphin is the symbol of the individual Christian, rather than of Christ himself, though in some instances the dolphin with the anchor seems to be intended as a representation of Christ upon the Cross." From *The Catholic Encyclopedia* (New York, 1909), *5*, 100. Compare

consolation to be derived from three great traditions; the first two, Judaic and Graeco-Roman, most clearly, and the third perhaps somewhat indirectly. Both images, of Michael and the Dolphins, are expressed in terms of Nature (for Michael is first and most emphatically St. Michael's Mount, and the Dolphins are likewise real), but move, by virtue of their symbolic resonance, beyond Nature. In some way Michael and the Dolphins are harbingers of the speaker, who next appears as bearer of good tidings. The speaker's turning to them, after contemplating the horror of Lycidas' weltering body, serves as a transition and permits his attitude to evolve from one of steady but grim despair to one, in Christian terms, of serene certainty.

Nature has been absolved of guilt; indeed, Nature, in various forms, has become one of the chief mourners. As we have noted before, there is a climactic succession of those concerned with the death of Lycidas: the plants, the Muses, the Nymphs. In the second section "universal Nature"—as rivers, springs, flowers, valleys—presides over the mourning which, through a kind of secondary climactic succession (Triton, Camus, Peter), becomes more and more formal and public. All the time, of course, the speaker was a mourner; but gradually he identified himself with others and left off speaking in the first person singular. Now, at the beginning of the third section, the mourners addressed for the first time [11] are those who, together with the speaker, were fictionally closest to Lycidas, namely, the Shepherds (poets or clerics):

"Gli antichi cristiani lo [i.e. the dolphin] hanno raffigurato con molta frequenza nelle iscrizioni del pesce (v.). Come pure si incontra sovente nelle lampade o nei portalampade, negli anelli e nei sigilli, ad es., con la scritta *spes in Deo* . . ." (*Enciclopedia Cattolica*, Vatican City, 1950, *4*, 1358). The "pesce" is of course a symbol of Christ.

11. There is a rather casual reference to the Shepherds in the passage which measures the loss of Lycidas in terms of Nature (lines 37–49): "Such, Lycidas, thy loss to Shepherd's ear" (line 49). It is Lycidas not necessarily as a person but as a poet.

> Weep no more, woeful Shepherds weep no more,
> For Lycidas your sorrow is not dead . . .

They come properly as the climax of personal mourning; and in a sense they constitute a public as the Nymphs did not. In two ways, then, the Shepherds are climactic: as personal mourners and as a public. But no sooner are they mentioned than they are told not to weep, that the cause of the sorrow is unreal. Lycidas is dead but not dead. Finally the Christian solution must be stated, and the paradox explained in Christian terms. As the speaker addresses the Shepherds, expounding the reason for joy, he is, in a sense, explaining it to himself. For in the previous part of the poem he has been gradually verging on the Christian truth, first exploring at length the pagan consolations and then, as if by discovery, coming upon the Christian answer. His Stoic attitude, developed gradually in pagan terms, is not incompatible with the new attitude of Christian consolation: it is both a bulwark against a recurrence of complete despair and a source of consolation for the irrevocable absence of Lycidas from earth.

Continuity with the foregoing part of the poem is preserved in several ways. As in the instances of Peter and Michael, there is a reluctance to use Christian names openly. It is, of course, clear that Lycidas has been raised from the dead by Christ and that he has gone to heaven. Still, neither Christ nor heaven is named; rather, the poem speaks only of "the dear might of him that walk'd the waves" and of a place "other groves, and other streams along." Also, Lycidas' resurrection is expressed in terms of Nature, the setting and the rising of the sun:

> . . . So sinks the day-star in the Ocean bed,
> And yet anon repairs his drooping head,
> And tricks his beams, and with new spangled Ore,
> Flames in the forehead of the morning sky . . .

Even the ocean, before passively cruel as the medium of Lycidas' death, becomes beneficent and practically a symbol of

God's grace through baptism and the whole scheme of re-demption.[12] The final reconciliation of pagan Nature, by now thoroughly benevolent, with the Christian world-view, by now well established, is achieved in the double figure of Lycidas as "saint" in heaven and "genius" on the shore. As the speaker explains the fullness of Lycidas' sainthood to the Shepherds, urging them as those most directly concerned (poets and clerics) to mourn no longer, he himself rises above grief and can turn directly to Lycidas, the final audience, and assure him that the mourners have ceased. Thus, the speaker's attitude has evolved so far, his certainty has become so great, that he can anticipate Lycidas' concern for the grief of his "friends." [13] His role has changed from that of mourner to that of universal comforter. What we have witnessed in the speaker, then, is a momentous change in attitude, beginning in reluctant introverted sorrow and ending in active public consolation. By a kind of gradual self-education the speaker, transcending one by one each partial resolution, has fully

12. It has been pointed out how the poem gains in structural tightness through the continuity of water imagery. In its various forms water represents both poetic inspiration and irremediable death; in the final resolution the water of God's grace enhances the water of poetic inspiration (Lycidas becomes not only one of the elect but also the "Genius of the shore") and nullifies the sinister water of death. See Maynard Mack, *Milton*, English Masterpieces, 4 (New York, 1950), 9–11; and J. E. Hardy, "Reconsideration I: Lycidas," *Kenyon Review*, 7 (1945), 99–113. Extravagances of interpretation in the second item have been toned down or eliminated in the essay on "Lycidas" in Cleanth Brooks and J. E. Hardy, *Poems of Mr. John Milton*, New York, 1952.

13. The change of audience from the Shepherds to Lycidas is not abrupt. If we accept the punctuation in the 1645 and 1673 editions, it is uncertain whether "Lycidas" in the line "Now Lycidas the Shepherds weep no more" is in the vocative or accusative case. It is true that in the first printing, in the collection of elegies on the death of Edward King, "Lycidas" is set off by commas. But the Trinity College Manuscript, like the definitive editions, omits them. See *John Milton's Complete Poetical Works*, ed. H. F. Fletcher (Urbana, 1943), *1*, 52 ff., 185 ff., 436 ff. All the editions and manuscripts are reproduced photographically. The ambiguity in the reading without commas allows an easier transition from audience to audience.

evolved his own attitude, always in terms of successive audiences and in terms of the reader. The gradualness of the evolution has been achieved in several important ways: the use of ambivalent symbols resonant in both pagan and Christian tradition (water, shepherding, dolphins, for instance); the use of contrasts and, more important, transitions; and, not to mention others, the climactic arrangement of audiences.

"Lycidas" can properly be viewed as a gradual reconciliation of Christian and pagan traditions. But it is necessary to see them reconciled in the course of the poem, as more and more is vouchsafed both speaker and reader. It is finally Christianity which at the climax supplies the only satisfactory answer. The speaker's terminal attitude of serene consolation is most fully expressed and justified in the lines

> . . . So Lycidas, sunk low, but mounted high,
> Through the dear might of him that walk'd the waves,

which are also the center, the point of resolution, of the time structure as I have analyzed it. Thus the first reading is confirmed. The central paradox is still Lycidas dead but not dead, sunk but risen; finally explained after partial explanations and finally brought into equilibrium through the "discovery" of Christian salvation.

At the end the speaker's role is complete; he has finished his performance and evolved his attitude. The audiences have played their successive or recurrent parts. And the reader has been activated to the extent of participating as witness in several places. Each rhetorical member has been developed in terms of the others. The whole rhetorical situation has, in a complex and unified way, been thoroughly exploited.

Yet a problem still remains: how to explain the last eight lines as a part of the rhetorical situation and as a part of the whole poem. Must we accept a new speaker, who refers to the previous speaker as an "uncouth Swain"?

> Thus sang the uncouth Swain to th'Oaks and rills,
> While the still morn went out with Sandals gray.

To some extent we must. But the switch is not by any means sudden. In evolving his attitude, the previous speaker has gradually made himself more and more impersonal or representative. It was in the nature of the function he assumed as celebrant or leader of mourning that he should increasingly take on a public or universal character. One might call it a process of self-objectification. In the last eight lines it is as if the speaker in his new position were looking back upon his earlier self. They serve, therefore, to objectify the original speaker by introducing a kind of superspeaker, an extrapolation of the first. In other ways the last eight lines catch up main threads and bind the poem. The whole process of mourning emerges more clearly as a formal public ceremony, celebrated by the speaker as performer.

> He touch't the tender stops of various Quills,
> With eager thought warbling his Doric lay.

Not only is the speaker put in perspective, but the reader is brought in again as final witness to a summary of the whole situation of the poem. No audience intrudes in this last stanza; it is all directed to the reader. Also, the dominant fiction of the poem, the pagan pastoral convention, reasserts itself, having now been reconciled with Christianity. There is no sense of strain, for the convention has not been broken. Rather, one might almost say that the Christian elements have been subdued in order to avoid any antagonism. And, finally, the last eight lines gather in references to time and place, which could be extracted from the main body of the poem and catalogued at length. A whole day has passed during the performance of the poem; when we are told that, we become more sharply aware of the gradualness with which the events of the poem have occurred. We are reminded, also, of the setting in which the poem takes place, for, having passed through several scattered localities (including the Irish Sea and heaven), we are back again in the original pastoral landscape. It could likewise be shown in greater detail how the rhetorical situation is more fully developed, how an effect of dramaticality is more forcefully achieved through the use of exclamations, questions, quotations, and interruptions. But even without exhaustive detail it is clear how the rhetorical structure is built and how it is related to the time structure and to the structure of images and ideas.

This, like the analysis of time structure, is only a partial analysis. To be anywhere near complete a full explication of the poem would have to include at least a coordinate discussion of imagery. In the present context, where our chief concern is to work toward a characterization of Baroque style, this partial analysis of "Lycidas" as a rhetorical structure at all events serves the important purpose of placing the poem (among the greatest achievements of the Baroque) in the major tradition. "Lycidas" is certainly one of the most complex examples of dramaticality through evolution of attitude. Both in that respect and in respect of time structure it stands as one of the most nearly complete fulfillments of peculiarly Baroque tendencies in style.

12. Summary

It can be safely said that none of the rhetorical devices used in Baroque poetry is entirely new; all of them, in one form or another, could be matched in Antiquity, in the Middle Ages and in the Renaissance. They seem, in fact, to be common aspects of spoken language.[1] For this reason, as I have urged before, we cannot speak of absolute invention: we must deal with configurations, tendencies, and trends. In the course of the several exegeses, which were designed to illustrate the Baroque use of the rhetorical situation, I have repeatedly referred to a general tendency toward what I called dramaticality. In part the exegeses themselves show proof of its existence. But also one should not fail to mention the total, less analyzable, impression derived from the several chief literatures of the time. In Italy the major lyric poets never freed themselves sufficiently from the Petrarchan tradition to allow full scope to new tendencies. All the same, there is—in some of the poems of Marino, for example—a new complexity, approaching evolution, of attitudes. Partly the new tone derives

1. One may draw the lesson from E. R. Curtius, *Europäische Literatur und lateinisches Mittelalter*, Bern, 1948; English version, New York, 1953.

from the tension set up between the old Petrarchan style and world-view and the new virtuosity and, one might almost say, cynicism. There was also a tendency to exploit suspense and surprise (one remembers Marino's dictum that the poet should strive to astound [2]) and to express the exaggerated and the grotesque. Turning to Spanish literature, the same tendencies are discoverable in Góngora and Quevedo, both of whom retained many of the Petrarchan conventions. Yet each made new departures, Góngora in his *romances* and longer poems, and Quevedo in his *romances* and *letrillas*. The attitudes expressed in their most original poems are often ironic or irreverent, assuming a convention and treating it lightly or freely: that is at least one way in which attitudes become complex and potentially evolutionary. As for French literature, one notices in several of the longer lyrics of Théophile and Saint-Amant a tendency to emphasize "performing" aspects: characterization of the speaker and gradualness. And to a marked degree, one notices an ability to delineate an evolution of attitude. In German literature the main tendency was somewhat freer of Petrarchan or Renaissance influence, though one cannot overlook the great number of pastorals and sonnets. It expressed itself characteristically in the full use of rhetorical devices (exclamations, questions, interruptions, asyndeton, etc.), which helped to create in many poems an intense effect of momentaneousness. In English literature all these tendencies, aspects of the new dramaticality, are to be found. The best lyrics of Donne and Milton fully and intricately exploit rhetorical devices to achieve gradualness and momentaneousness and a high degree of particularization and characterization. In every na-

2.   È del poeta il fin la meraviglia
           (parlo de l'eccellente e non del goffo):
           chi non sa far stupir, vada alla striglia!

This is the first tercet of Sonnet xx in the *Murtoleide*, a sonnet sequence attacking the poet Gaspare Murtola. For the context, see *Poesie varie* ed. Croce, p. 395.

tional tradition, of course, there are poets of lesser stature who would have to be discussed in a full survey.

These, then, are generalizations which at least characterize a limited but crucial sampling. If one were to generalize further, trying to comprehend *all* discernible tendencies in the Baroque lyric, one would probably end by making true but hardly significant statements about poetry in general. Let the broadest generalization be that in the Baroque lyric there is a strong tendency which we have called dramaticality, and that its most advanced form is an evolution of attitudes.

At least in passing it should be mentioned that the Baroque age is the high point in the development of the modern European theater. Since we define the word "baroque" in such a way as to dispel its former pejorative associations, we should have little reluctance to see the term applied to Corneille and Racine. Shakespeare is more difficult. Though he is clearly a borderline figure between Renaissance and Baroque, his influence on his age was in every way on the Baroque side.[3] Likewise, there are Baroque traits in Lope which become more accentuated in his followers, such as Calderón, Tirso, and Alarcón. The point of interest in all this is the fact that the theater did flourish in modern Europe as never before. Undoubtedly the same conditions that brought the theater to its apogee also brought the lyric to its. Yet it seems likely that they not only developed in parallel fashion but that the one influenced the other; and it is most likely that the theater influenced the lyric. I refer, of course, not to the lyric imbedded in a play, which is usually slight, at least out of context, but rather to the independent lyric, which more and more concerned itself with complexities.

In the series of poems just analyzed there is a kind of double progression: each national tradition offers us poems

3. See the very interesting article by Marco Mincoff, "Baroque Literature in England," *Annuaire de l'Université de Sofia: Faculté Historico-Philologique,* *43* (1946–47), 3–71. It is actually concerned with Beaumont and Fletcher, and claims that the latter is the first Baroque dramatist in Europe.

which increase, from Italy to England, in complexity. The progression in terms of national tradition, while roughly correct, would have to be argued and qualified. More important in the present context is the fact that the poems analyzed, notwithstanding their diverse provenience, have in common a strong tendency toward dramaticality. In the sonnet of Gryphius dramaticality showed itself most strikingly in the use of minor devices to create an effect of immediate address and momentaneousness. Still, the rhetorical situation remained somewhat vague and undeveloped. Marino's "Canzone" represented an advance in complexity: to some extent the speaker and audience were characterized; there were signs of a developing attitude in the speaker. But the poem relied too much on a rather static contrast between idealized and cynical love.

Something of that same contrast was found in Théophile's "La Solitude"; the main source of dramaticality, however, was the relationship between the speaker and his beloved, which was evolved in terms of the speaker's attitude toward a succession of audiences. The minor devices were subordinated to the development of the rhetorical situation. Especially in Donne's poems did we find examples of a remarkably full use of the rhetorical situation, in terms of a gradual yet extensive evolution of attitude. A large measure of the complexity achieved was due to the great breadth of the gamut through which the evolution of attitude ran. His openings were not egotistical shock tactics but rather artistically controlled outbursts appropriate to fictional characters. It was, in fact, part of Donne's genius that he succeeded in finding a way, in the course of a poem, to reconcile the extremes of opening and close: he discovered, we might say, a diplomatic formula or a way to bend without breaking.

Even more than Donne's poems, Milton's "Lycidas" is a performance. The speaker characterizes himself as a performer or, better, the celebrant of a public ritual. But that, happily, does not enforce upon him a static characterization, for he is also a mourner with the rest. From the first, his characterization evolves in terms of a tension between his roles as celebrant, who gradually becomes omniscient (it is also he who bears the good tidings), and mourner, who passes through stages of grief and resignation to reach final serenity. His attitude evolves in a most complex way, working out not only his own serenity but also a reconciliation of two intricate and momentous traditions.

In defining Baroque dramaticality, my central concern has been the rhetorical situation; but one should not, of course, neglect rhetorical devices, whose use in the Baroque provides a key to the most fruitful and original discoveries. Nor should one neglect the growing ability to embrace disparates, to take the alternative into account. Already examples have been given, in the Gongorine formulas or in epicedes which pretend that the deceased is not dead. And the analyses provide further instances. Gryphius' "Der Tod" implies the choice between attachment to worldly things and preparation for death. In Marino's "Canzone" love and lust are assumed to be bound up in one another; but it is a rather flimsy confusion, not, as in Donne, a synthesis, through the body to the soul. The process of taking alternatives into account becomes more intimately associated with the rhetorical structure in the analyzed poems of Théophile, Donne, and Milton. For in each instance the initial attitude of the speaker is an alternative to the final attitude; and the first is subsumed, most successfully of course in Donne and Milton, in the second.

The full argument would lead on beyond a consideration of the immediate rhetorical situation to questions of imagery and the cultivation of the grotesque. More generally, as I have said before, the development of dramaticality in the Baroque lyric suggests some relation to the contemporaneous flowering of the theater, which, in the figures of Lope, Shakespeare, and Corneille, was so extraordinarily quick to mature in complexity. These and other trends, such as the mixture of styles, are undoubtedly interrelated. How and to what degree would need a long answer. For the present it is enough to conclude, on the basis of limited yet detailed evidence, that some of the very best Baroque lyrics derived great strength of structure from the original way in which they exploited the rhetorical situation. Never before had the lyric achieved so conspicuous a degree of complexity and dramaticality. It is not surprising that the lyric, now so highly developed, should go into decline for want of a surpassing genius.

IV. A SPECULATIVE CONCLUSION

Those who speak of the Baroque style in poetry as decadence or disease are guilty of a number of misconceptions. Usually they make Baroque too narrow and find it only in the most extravagant works of poets like Marino, Crashaw, or Góngora; and usually they define Baroque only in terms of the conceit or other rhetorical devices. But once we make it a period concept and test it without prejudice against the total style of the age, we discover that isolated extravagances are often manifestations of a broader tendency than we might have imagined. During the Baroque age, the greatest poets discovered new and original techniques for structuring poetry and enabling it to express complexities. Conceit and metaphor were not new means of structure but part of the traditional resources of the poet. If they were used extravagantly in Baroque poetry, the same can be said of other periods in the history of literature. It has not yet been shown precisely what characterized their use in the Baroque. Looking elsewhere, we find that new means of structure and complexity can be discovered in universal elements of poetry which before had been taken for granted: in time and drama.

The use of time as a means of structure was part of a broader tendency to view time under the aspect of eternity as contingent and manipulatable. It is an ancient commonplace to say that time flies or crawls, according to the way one feels; "subjective" time designates a universal human experience. But to think of time in relation to eternity is to enter into a realm of speculation full of paradox. Christian theologians were used to thinking in such terms, yet poets were not.[1] Time in poetry, as expressed in tense and temporal reference, had not been actively exploited as a conspicuous means of structure. It was in the Baroque age that poets first took up the notion of time viewed through eternity and found that its paradoxical nature admitted liberties that common sense and subjective time did not. In this way we can explain, in terms of the history of ideas, what at first seems an odd and extravagant use of time. The whole tendency, as reflected in poetry, reached its culmination in those lyrics which use time as a conspicuous means of structure. Poetically, the drastic tense changes in the "Nativity Ode," for example, can be seen as a major part of the total structure of the poem; indeed, they reinforce its whole ideology. It is significant both for the history of poetic style and for the history of ideas that time is used as a conspicuous means of structure in poems as diverse as the "Polifemo," the "Nativity Ode," and "Lycidas." It is a characteristic of Baroque poetry in general, not merely of one national tradition. True, it found its best expression in England and Spain, but that is not surprising, since those countries produced the best lyrics of the age. Moreover, the same tendency is evident in other countries.

Drama, conceived of as the interaction between rhetorical members in a poem, is also related to universal human experience. Relationships between human beings create attitudes and characterize individuals. Complex states of mind, of course, existed in reality long before they were represented in imaginative literature. If we should posit a tradition whose exemplars are Catullus, Petrarch, and Ronsard, we could perhaps infer a developing ability to express complex attitudes in the lyric. Our tradition would culminate in

1. Doctrinally, of course, Dante was well aware of the difficulties of expressing eternal things in temporal terms: "Trasumanar significar *per verba* / Non si poria; però l'essemplo basti / A cui esperïenza grazia serba" (*Paradiso*, I, 70–72).

the Baroque, when the usual means for achieving dramaticality were conspicuously exploited, and a new means, dramaticality through an evolution of attitudes, was discovered. All national traditions did not attain a true evolution of attitudes. Yet the general tendency was stronger in the direction of dramaticality than it had been before. If we take the explicated poems in the order in which they were discussed, we will have a rough notion of the relative importance of each national tradition. There is a line of development, out of time, from Gryphius to Marino to Théophile to Donne to Milton ("Lycidas"). Rhetorical devices—asyndeton, exclamations, direct discourse—are used with considerable intensity by Gryphius and Marino, as also by their followers in Germany and Italy. Théophile, and we might also say Saint-Amant and Tristan l'Hermite, achieves a sort of simple evolution of attitudes. But it remained for the English, Donne and Milton, not to mention Vaughan or Marvell, to make full use of the rhetorical situation in creating a complex evolution of attitudes. Before the Baroque, complex *ideas* had, of course, been expressed in the lyric. One need only recall Dante's three *canzoni* which he himself explicates so tortuously in the *Convivio*. But never before had complex *attitudes* been evolved gradually as a main part of the structure of a poem.

Both time and drama, then, were means of unity and complexity for the Baroque lyric. We might go further and say that the two tendencies, toward time as manipulatable and toward dramaticality, may be seen as part of a more general trend toward particularization. A poem whose structure is partially determined by the fusing of disjunct time planes or by the characterization of rhetorical members could be considered more particularized than one whose structure is not so determined. To draw an analogy from mathematics: a point is particularized in a plane by two coordinates; three coordinates particularize it in three-dimensional space; and four particularize it further in time. A point, then, is most fully particularized, in such a system, when it has all four coordinates. Similarly, poetic structure may be said to be most fully particularized when it is determined by structural time and drama, together with imagery, meter, and other lesser elements. Rhetorical devices, specification of place, and narrative time must be taken into account as well; but they are certainly not major coordinates. What I have called gradualness and momentaneousness could be considered effects or concomitants of particularization. In most general terms, the tone of directness and immediacy in the best Baroque poety derives from the same source or works to the same end.

Properly to relate the new structural use of time and drama to the history of ideas and to literary history as a whole, would take a lengthy exposition. On the surface there seem to be two conflicting tendencies. The new rationalism did not necessarily accept the orthodox Christian view of time and eternity, but, at least indirectly, subjected it to the same scrutiny as it had epistemology. At the same time a sort of antirationalism, including mystics and pietists, tried to escape the question by making time unreal and illusory. Thus, as the old orthodoxy lost its supremacy, new ways of looking at time became possible. Since time was no longer taken for granted, it could enter the active repertory of poetic techniques: it could be manipulated by the poet. Góngora and Milton attempted the identification of separate time planes; and Gryphius, using every means to minimize the "temporality" of his medium, even attempted to describe events outside of time. In some such way drama, too, could be related to the history of ideas. With the break-up of the old order, new sources of complexity and tension became available to the poet. To have any sort of world-view it was necessary to have a relatively complex one. Not only that, it became increasingly necessary to include in the lyric more and more of an adequate world-view, since none could be taken completely for granted. Furthermore, we should again observe that in science there was a questioning of Aristotelian motion and a concern for empirical particulars; and that in literature there was an extraordinary development in the theater.

Fortunately the growing complexity of an adequate world-view was paralleled by a growing technical mastery to cope with it in the lyric. It would be difficult to say whether one was cause and the other effect. At all events, the range of poetic material was immensely widened and the means for expressing it were discovered. Poetic material came to include what in the Renaissance would have been considered improprieties or extravagances in serious poetry. To some extent, undoubtedly, far-fetched metaphors or ingenious schemes of structure were exercises in virtuosity, calculated to astound. But on the whole they seem to have been attempts, successful and unsuccessful, to find objective correlatives for complex emotions new to the lyric.[2] Many of Donne's poems, for example, can be seen as complex studies of lovers' psychology. A lover very much in love can affect cynicism or pretend not to care; he can look at himself objectively and still play the lovesick fool. Donne achieves a complexity, adumbrated in Marino and Théophile, which cannot be reduced to simple anti-Petrarchism or conventional naturalism.

The lyrics analyzed were discussed, purely as examples of poetic style, in both historical and national terms. Not only do they show basic similarities in style, but they occur within the compass of less than a hundred years. It is their stylistic and historical coherence that enables us to call them all Baroque. They also belong to five national traditions—different, yet having largely the same heritage and subject to largely the same ideological influences. For these reasons we can set

---

2. For the sake of completeness, there is no need to rule out the possibility that they were also attempts to find complex emotions through new juxtapositions and techniques. But this possibility does not necessarily furnish grounds for the usual charges of coldness or shallowness or infatuation with words.

them in the same international tradition, and posit Baroque as a European movement. Though my first concern was to characterize aspects of Baroque style in itself, I have also tried to suggest concrete comparisons with the Renaissance lyric. To be exhaustive, of course, one would have to analyze at length the means of structure peculiar to the Renaissance lyric and show in detail how different it is from structure in the Baroque lyric. But in order to characterize fully Renaissance lyric style, it would be necessary to set it off from style in the medieval and classical lyric. The process might become hopelessly retrogressive. The only practical alternative, therefore, is to leap into the middle of things. But we must never lose sight of the full scope of literary history. Taking that for granted, the literary historian is concerned first of all with defining the dominant stylistic tendency of a period and recording its vicissitudes. His way of determining it is to discover the characteristics of style common to the best works. Then he can proceed to arrange lesser tendencies in their proper perspective. For example, we cannot but acknowledge the fact that throughout the Baroque a huge quantity of verse was written in the most workaday Renaissance style. Most of the anacreontic, pastoral, or occasional verse counts for very little. Some of it is merely competent and some of it approaches the style of the great poems. It may be called Baroque in that it was written during the Baroque period or in that it shows Baroque traits of style, but it does not affect the definition of Baroque style. We should not feel obliged, then, to account for every poem. We should be content to find ways of distinguishing between the styles of great poems.

Among its other limitations, my contribution to defining Baroque lyric style neglects treating imagery. It has not yet been shown how any meaningful distinction can be made between Baroque imagery and the imagery of other styles.[3]

3. See Rosemond Tuve, *Elizabethan and Metaphysical Imagery* (Chicago, 1947), and Leonard Unger, *Donne's Poetry and Modern Criticism* (Chicago, 1950), now reprinted in his *The Man in the Name* (Minneapolis, 1956).

Meanwhile, time and drama seem to me adequate ways of characterizing Baroque style in the lyric. As conspicuous means of structure, they were virtually discoveries of the Baroque. At the close of the Baroque, the lyric as a developing genre had, for a time, run its course. When it was revived again in the later eighteenth century, its nature had greatly changed.

TEXTS

John Milton: "On the Morning of Christ's Nativity"

1

This is the Month, and this the happy morn
Wherein the Son of Heav'n's eternal King,
Of wedded Maid, and Virgin Mother born,
Our great redemption from above did bring;
For so the holy sages once did sing,
    That he our deadly forfeit should release,
And with his Father work us a perpetual peace.

2

That glorious Form, that Light unsufferable,
And that far-beaming blaze of Majesty,
Wherewith he wont at Heav'n's high Council-Table,
To sit the midst of Trinal Unity,
He laid aside; and here with us to be,
    Forsook the Courts of everlasting Day,
And chose with us a darksome House of mortal Clay.

3

Say Heav'nly Muse, shall not thy sacred vein
Afford a present to the Infant God?
Hast thou no verse, no hymn, or solemn strain,
To welcome him to this his new abode,
Now while the Heav'n by the Sun's team untrod,
    Hath took no print of the approaching light,
And all the spangled host keep watch in squadrons bright?

4

See how from far upon the Eastern road
The Star-led Wizards haste with odours sweet:
O run, prevent them with thy humble ode,
And lay it lowly at his blessed feet;
Have thou the honour first, thy Lord to greet,
    And join thy voice unto the Angel Quire,
From out his secret Altar toucht with hallow'd fire.

The Hymn

1

It was the Winter wild,
While the Heav'n-born child,
    All meanly wrapt in the rude manger lies;
Nature in awe to him
Had doff't her gaudy trim,
    With her great Master so to sympathize:
It was no season then for her
To wanton with the Sun, her lusty Paramour.

2

Only with speeches fair
She woos the gentle Air
    To hide her guilty front with innocent Snow,
And on her naked shame,
Pollute with sinful blame,
    The Saintly Veil of Maiden white to throw,
Confounded, that her Maker's eyes
Should look so near upon her foul deformities.

3

But he her fears to cease,
Sent down the meek-ey'd Peace;
    She crown'd with Olive green, came softly sliding
Down through the turning sphere,
His ready Harbinger,

With Turtle wing the amorous clouds dividing,
And waving wide her myrtle wand,
She strikes a universal Peace through Sea and Land.

4

No War, or Battle's sound
Was heard the World around,
    The idle spear and shield were high up hung;
The hooked Chariot stood
Unstain'd with hostile blood;
    The Trumpet spake not to the armed throng,
And Kings sat still with awful eye,
As if they surely knew their sovran Lord was by.

5

But peaceful was the night
Wherein the Prince of light
    His reign of peace upon the earth began:
The Winds, with wonder whist,
Smoothly the waters kiss't,
    Whispering new joys to the mild Ocean,
Who now hath quite forgot to rave,
While Birds of Calm sit brooding on the charmed wave.

6

The Stars with deep amaze
Stand fixt in steadfast gaze,
    Bending one way their precious influence,
And will not take their flight,
For all the morning light,
    Or *Lucifer* that often warn'd them thence;
But in their glimmering Orbs did glow,
Until their Lord himself bespake, and bid them go.

7

And though the shady gloom
Had given day her room,
    The Sun himself withheld his wonted speed,

And hid his head for shame,
As his inferior flame,
  The new enlight'n'd world no more should need;
He saw a greater Sun appear
Than his bright Throne, or burning Axletree could bear.

8

The Shepherds on the Lawn,
Or ere the point of dawn,
  Sat simply chatting in a rustic row;
Full little thought they than,
That the mighty *Pan*
  Was kindly come to live with them below;
Perhaps their loves, or else their sheep,
Was all that did their silly thoughts so busy keep.

9

When such music sweet
Their hearts and ears did greet,
  As never was by mortal finger strook,
Divinely-warbled voice
Answering the stringed noise,
  As all their souls in blissful rapture took:
The Air such pleasure loth to lose,
With thousand echoes still prolongs each heav'nly close.

10

Nature that heard such sound
Beneath the hollow round
  Of *Cynthia's* seat, the Airy region thrilling,
Now was almost won
To think her part was done,
  And that her reign had here its last fulfilling;
She knew such harmony alone
Could hold all Heav'n and Earth in happier union.

11

At last surrounds their sight
A Globe of circular light,

That with long beams the shame-fac't night array'd,
The helmed Cherubim
And sworded Seraphim
Are seen in glittering ranks with wings display'd,
Harping in loud and solemn quire,
With unexpressive notes to Heav'n's new-born Heir.

12

Such Music (as 'tis said)
Before was never made,
But when of old the sons of morning sung,
While the Creator Great
His constellations set,
And the well-balanc't world on hinges hung,
And cast the dark foundations deep,
And bid the welt'ring waves their oozy channel keep.

13

Ring out ye Crystal spheres,
Once bless our human ears,
(If ye have power to touch our senses so)
And let your silver chime
Move in melodious time;
And let the Bass of Heav'n's deep Organ blow;
And with your ninefold harmony
Make up full consort to th'Angelic symphony.

14

For if such holy Song
Enwrap our fancy long,
Time will run back, and fetch the age of gold,
And speckl'd vanity
Will sicken soon and die,
And leprous sin will melt from earthly mould,
And Hell itself will pass away,
And leave her dolorous mansions to the peering day.

15

Yea, Truth and Justice then
Will down return to men,

Th'enamel'd *Arras* of the Rain-bow wearing,
And Mercy set between,
Thron'd in Celestial sheen,
    With radiant feet the tissued clouds down steering,
And Heav'n as at some festival,
Will open wide the Gates of her high Palace Hall.

16

But wisest Fate says no,
This must not yet be so,
    The Babe lies yet in smiling Infancy,
That on the bitter cross
Must redeem our loss;
    So both himself and us to glorify:
Yet first to those ychain'd in sleep,
The wakeful trump of doom must thunder through the deep,

17

With such a horrid clang
As on mount *Sinai* rang
    While the red fire, and smould'ring clouds out brake:
The aged Earth aghast
With terror of that blast,
    Shall from the surface to the centre shake,
When at the world's last session,
The dreadful Judge in middle Air shall spread his throne.

18

And then at last our bliss
Full and perfect is,
    But now begins; for from this happy day
Th'old Dragon under ground,
In straiter limits bound,
    Not half so far casts his usurped sway,
And wrath to see his Kingdom fail,
Swinges the scaly Horror of his folded tail.

19

The Oracles are dumb,
No voice or hideous hum

Runs through the arched roof in words deceiving.
Apollo from his shrine
Can no more divine,
  With hollow shriek the steep of *Delphos* leaving.
No nightly trance, or breathed spell,
Inspires the pale-ey'd Priest from the prophetic cell.

20

The lonely mountains o'er,
And the resounding shore,
  A voice of weeping heard, and loud lament;
From haunted spring and dale
Edg'd with poplar pale,
  The parting Genius is with sighing sent;
With flow'r-inwov'n tresses torn
The Nymphs in twilight shade of tangled thickets mourn.

21

In consecrated Earth,
And on the holy Hearth,
  The *Lars,* and *Lemures* moan with midnight plaint;
In Urns and Altars round,
A drear and dying sound
  Affrights the *Flamens* at their service quaint;
And the chill Marble seems to sweat,
While each peculiar power forgoes his wonted seat.

22

Peor and *Baalim*
Forsake their Temples dim,
  With that twice-batter'd god of *Palestine,*
And mooned *Ashtaroth,*
Heav'n's Queen and Mother both,
  Now sits not girt with Tapers' holy shine,
The Libyc *Hammon* shrinks his horn,
In vain the *Tyrian* Maids their wounded *Thammuz* mourn.

23

And Sullen *Moloch,* fled,
Hath left in shadows dread

His burning Idol all of blackest hue;
In vain with Cymbals' ring
They call the grisly king,
   In dismal dance about the furnace blue;
The brutish gods of *Nile* as fast,
Isis and *Orus,* and the Dog *Anubis* haste.

24

Nor is *Osiris* seen
In *Memphian* Grove or Green,
   Trampling the unshow'r'd Grass with lowings loud:
Nor can he be at rest
Within his sacred chest,
   Naught but profoundest Hell can be his shroud:
In vain with Timbrel'd Anthems dark
The sable-stoled Sorcerers bear his worshipt Ark.

25

He feels from *Juda's* Land
The dreaded Infant's hand,
   The rays of *Bethlehem* blind his dusky eyn;
Nor all the gods beside,
Longer dare abide,
   Nor *Typhon* huge ending in snaky twine:
Our Babe, to show his Godhead true,
Can in his swaddling bands control the damned crew.

26

So when the Sun in bed,
Curtain'd with cloudy red,
   Pillows his chin upon an Orient wave,
The flocking shadows pale
Troop to th'infernal jail;
   Each fetter'd Ghost slips to his several grave,
And the yellow-skirted *Fays*
Fly after the Night-steeds, leaving their Moon-lov'd maze.

27

But see! the Virgin blest,
Hath laid her Babe to rest.

Time is our tedious Song should here have ending;
Heav'n's youngest teemed Star
Hath fixt her polisht Car,
Her sleeping Lord with Handmaid Lamp attending:
And all about the Courtly Stable,
Bright-harness'd Angels sit in order serviceable.

Luis de Góngora y Argote:
"Fábula de Polifemo y Galatea"

Al Conde de Niebla

(1)

Estas que me dictó, rimas sonoras,
culta sí, aunque bucólica Talía,
oh, excelso Conde, en las purpúreas horas
que es rosas la alba y rosicler el día,
ahora que de luz tu Niebla doras,
escucha, al son de la zampoña mía,
si ya los muros no te ven de Huelva
peinar el viento, fatigar la selva.

(2)

Templado pula en la maestra mano
el generoso pájaro su pluma,
o tan mudo en la alcándara, que en vano
aun desmentir al cascabel presuma;
tascando haga el freno de oro cano
del caballo andaluz la ociosa espuma;
gima el lebrel en el cordón de seda,
y al cuerno al fin la cítara suceda.

(3)

Treguas al ejercicio sean robusto,
ocio atento, silencio dulce, en cuanto
debajo escuchas de dosel augusto
del músico jayán el fiero canto.

Luis de Góngora y Argote:
"Fable of Polifemus and Galatea"
To the Conde de Niebla

(1)

These sonorous rimes which cultured, yes, though bucolic Thalia dictated to me, O noble Count, in the reddening hours when dawn is roses and the day rose-bright, now that you gild your "mist" with light, hear, to the sound of my pipes, as the walls of Huelva no longer see you comb the wind, vex the forest.

(2)

Tempered, in the masterful hand, let the noble bird polish its plumes, or let it, so mute on its perch, attempt in vain to belie its bell; let the leisurely foam of the grazing Andalusian horse make hoary the golden bridle; let the hound groan on the silken cord, and to the cithara at last let the horn give way.

(3)

Let there be a truce with the robust regimen, attentive leisure, sweet silence, while beneath an august canopy you listen to the wild song of the musical giant. Today taste changes with the Muses, but if mine can offer a sufficient

Alterna con las Musas hoy el gusto,
que si la mía puede ofrecer tanto
clarín, y de la Fama no segundo,
tu nombre oirán los términos del mundo.

* * *

1

Donde espumoso el mar sicilïano
el pie argenta de plata al Lilibeo,
bóveda o de las fraguas de Vulcano
o tumba de los huesos de Tifeo,
pálidas señas cenizoso un llano,
cuando no de el sacrílego deseo,
de el duro oficio da. Allí una alta roca
mordaza es a una gruta de su boca.

2

Guarnición tosca de este escollo duro
troncos robustos son, a cuya greña
menos luz debe, menos aire puro
la caverna profunda, que a la peña;
caliginoso lecho, el seno obscuro
ser de la negra noche nos lo enseña
infame turba de nocturnas aves,
gimiendo tristes y volando graves.

3

De este, pues, formidable de la tierra
bostezo, el melancólico vacío
a Polifemo, horror de aquella sierra,
bárbara choza es, albergue umbrío,
y redil espacioso donde encierra
cuanto las cumbres ásperas, cabrío,
de los montes esconde: copia bella
que un silbo junta y un peñasco sella.

trumpet (and not Fame's second) the ends of the earth shall hear your name.

* * *

1

Where the foaming Sicilian sea silvers the foot of the Lily-baean, either vault of Vulcan's forges or tomb of Typhaeus' bones, an ashen plain, if not of sacrilegious desire, gives pale signs of the grim occupation. There a high rock is a gag to the mouth of a grotto.

2

Rugged garrison of these stern shoals are robust trunks, to whose elflocks the deep cavern owes less light, less pure air, than to the cliff; the nefarious flock of night birds, gloomily groaning and heavily flying, shows us that it, a caliginous bed, is the dark recess of the black night.

3

Now, the melancholy emptiness of this fearful yawn of the earth is for Polyphemus, terror of that range, a barbarous hut, shadowy dwelling and spacious sheepfold, where he encloses such a herd as hides the rough peaks of the mountains: a seemly plenty which a whistle gathers and a boulder seals in.

4

Un monte era de miembros eminente
éste que, de Neptuno hijo fiero,
de un ojo ilustra el orbe de su frente,
émulo casi de el mayor lucero;
cíclope a quien el pino más valiente,
bastón, le obedecía tan ligero,
y al grave peso junco tan delgado
que un día era bastón y otro cayado.

5

Negro el cabello, imitador undoso
de las obscuras aguas de el Leteo,
al viento que le peina proceloso
vuela sin orden, pende sin aseo;
un torrente es su barba impetüoso
que, adusto hijo de este Pirineo,
su pecho inunda, o tarde o mal o en vano
surcada aún de los dedos de su mano.

6

No la Trinacria en sus montañas, fiera
armó de crüeldad, calzó de viento,
que redima feroz, salve ligera,
su piel manchada de colores ciento:
pellico es ya la que en los bosques era
mortal horror, al que con paso lento
los bueyes a su albergue reducía,
pisando la dudosa luz de el día.

7

Cercado es, cuanto más capaz más lleno,
de la fruta, el zurrón, casi abortada,
que el tardo Otoño deja al blando seno
de la piadosa yerba encomendada:
la serba, a quien le da rugas el heno;
la pera, de quien fué cuna dorada
la rubia paja, y, pálida tutora,
la niega avara y pródiga la dora.

4

A mountain he was, lofty of limb, who, wild son of Neptune, illumines with one eye the orb of his forehead, nearly rivaling the greater light; cyclops whom the most valiant pine tree obeyed, a stock so light and a reed for the heavy bulk so slender that one day it was a stock, and another, a shepherd's crook.

5

His black hair, wavy imitator of the dark waters of Lethe, flies disorderly in the gusty wind that combs it, hangs uncleanly; his beard is an impetuous torrent, which, sunscorched offspring of this Pyrenee, inundates his breast, constantly furrowed, either too late or badly or in vain, by the fingers of his hand.

6

Trinacria, in her mountains, did not arm with cruelty, shoe with wind, any beast that could fiercely redeem, fleetly save its skin stained with a hundred colors: what in the woods was a deathly terror is a doublet now for him who with slow step led back the oxen to his dwelling, treading the doubtful light of day.

7

Fortified is the shepherd's pouch, the more capacious the more filled, with fruit almost abortive, which late Autumn commends to the mild bosom of the pious grass: the sorbapple whom the hay wrinkles; the pear whose gilded cradle was the yellow straw, which, pale protectress, hides it greedily and gilds it prodigally.

8

Erizo es, el zurrón, de la castaña;
y, entre el membrillo o verde o datilado,
de la manzana hipócrita, que engaña
a lo pálido no, a lo arrebolado;
y de la encina, honor de la montaña
que pabellón al siglo fué dorado,
el tributo, alimento, aunque grosero,
de el mejor mundo, de el candor primero.

9

Cera y cáñamo unió, que no debiera,
cient cañas, cuyo bárbaro ruído,
de más ecos que unió cáñamo y cera
albogues, duramente es repetido.
La selva se confunde, el mar se altera,
rompe Tritón su caracol torcido,
sordo huye el bajel a vela y remo:
¡tal la música es de Polifemo!

10

Ninfa, de Doris hija, la más bella,
adora, que vió el reino de la espuma.
Galatea es su nombre, y dulce en ella
el terno Venus de sus gracias suma.
Son una y otra luminosa estrella
lucientes ojos de su blanca pluma:
si roca de cristal no es de Neptuno,
pavón de Venus es, cisne de Juno.

11

Purpúreas rosas sobre Galatea
la Alba entre lilios cándidos deshoja;
duda el Amor cuál más su color sea,
O púrpura nevada, o nieve roja.
De su frente la perla es, Eritrea,
émula vana. El ciego Dios se enoja
y condenado su esplendor, la deja
pender en oro al nácar de su oreja.

8

The shepherd's pouch is a prickly shell to the chestnut and
to the hypocritical apple—quince half green or date-colored
—that deceives not in being pale but in being crimson; and
to the offering of the oak—honor of the mountain, which
for the golden age was a pavilion—food, though coarse, for
the best world, for the primal innocence.

9

Wax and hemp joined, as they should not, a hundred reeds,
whose barbarous noise is harshly repeated in more echoes
than the pipes that hemp and wax joined. The forest is perplexed, the sea is troubled, Triton breaks his twisted shell,
deaf flies the ship by sail and oar: such is the music of
Polyphemus.

10

He worships a nymph, the loveliest of Doris' daughters, who
saw the kingdom of the foam. Galatea is her name, and
gentle Venus leads in her the triad of her graces. The one and
the other luminous star are the sparkling eyes of her white
plumage: if she is not Neptune's crystal rock, she is Venus'
peacock, Juno's swan.

11

Among white lilies the Dawn scatters red roses over Galatea.
Love doubts which is more her hew, snowy crimson, or red
snow. The Eritrean pearl is vain rival of her brow. The blind
god is angered and, condemning its brilliance, lets it hang in
gold from the mother-of-pearl of her ear.

12

Invidia de las Ninfas y cuidado
de cuantas honra el mar, deidades, era;
pompa de el marinero niño alado
que sin fanal conduce su venera.
Verde el cabello, el pecho no escamado,
ronco sí, escucha a Glauco la ribera
inducir a pisar la bella ingrata,
en carro de cristal, campos de plata.

13

Marino joven, las cerúleas sienes
de el más tierno coral ciñe Palemo,
rico de cuantos la agua engendra bienes
de el Faro odioso al Promontorio extremo;
mas en la gracia igual, si en los desdenes
perdonado algo más que Polifemo,
de la que aun no le oyó y, calzada plumas,
tantas flores pisó como él espumas.

14

Huye la ninfa bella, y el marino
amante nadador ser bien quisiera,
ya que no áspid a su pie divino,
dorado pomo a su veloz carrera.
Mas, ¿cuál diente mortal, cuál metal fino
la fuga suspender podrá ligera
que el desdén solicita? ¡Oh, cuánto yerra
delfín que sigue en agua corza en tierra!

15

Sicilia, en cuanto oculta, en cuanto ofrece,
copa es de Baco, huerto de Pomona:
tanto de frutas ésta la enriquece
cuanto aquél de racimos la corona.
En carro que estival trillo parece,
a sus campañas Ceres no perdona,
de cuyas siempre fértiles espigas
las provincias de Europa son hormigas.

12

She was the envy of the nymphs and the concern of as many
deities as the sea honors; pomp of the sea-going winged boy
who lanternless steers his shell. Green his hair and his breast
unscaly, but hoarse, he listens to Glaucus persuading the
lovely ingrate to tread on the beach, in crystal chariot, on
fields of silver.

13

Marine youth, Palemus circles his sky-blue temples with the
tenderest coral, rich in as many goods as the water engenders,
from the hateful Pharos to the farthest Promontory; but
equal in the graces, if somewhat more forgiven than Polyphemus in the disdainings of her who never listened to him
and who, shod with feathers, trod as many flowers as he did
bubbles.

14

The lovely nymph flees, and the marine lover would very
much like to be a swimmer, if not an asp to her divine foot,
a golden apple to her swift course. But what fatal tooth, what
fine metal could suspend the fleet escape disdain arouses?
O how astray is the dolphin that follows in water the antelope
on land!

15

Sicily, in what it hides, in what it offers, is Bacchus' chalice,
Pomona's garden: by as much fruit she enriches it as he
with grape-clusters crowns it. In a chariot that seems a
summer thresher, Ceres does not pardon its fields, to whose
ever fruitful sheaves the provinces of Europe are ants.

16

A Pales su viciosa cumbre debe
lo que a Ceres, y aun más su vega llana;
pues si en la una granos de oro llueve,
copos nieva en la otra mil de lana.
De cuantos siegan oro, esquilan nieve,
o en pipas guardan la exprimida grana,
bien sea religión, bien amor sea,
deidad, aunque sin templo, es Galatea.

17

Sin aras no: que el margen donde para
del espumoso mar su pie ligero,
al labrador de sus primicias ara,
de sus esquilmos es al ganadero;
de la copia a la tierra poco avara
el cuerno vierte el hortelano entero
sobre la mimbre que tejió prolija,
si artificiosa no, su honesta hija.

18

Arde la juventud, y los arados
peinan las tierras que surcaron antes,
mal conducidos, cuando no arrastrados,
de tardos bueyes cual su dueño errantes;
sin pastor que los silbe, los ganados
los crujidos ignoran resonantes
de las hondas, si en vez del pastor pobre
el Céfiro no silba, o cruje el robre.

19

Mudo la noche el can, el día dormido,
de cerro en cerro y sombra en sombra yace,
Bala el ganado; al mísero balido,
nocturno el lobo de las sombras nace:
cébase, y fiero deja humecido
en sangre de una lo que la otra pace.
¡Revoca, Amor, los silbos, o a su dueño
el silencio del can siga y el sueño!

16

The luxuriant highland owes to Pales what its level plain
owes to Ceres, and even more: for if on the one place it rains
pellets of gold, on the other it snows woolly flakes. Of those
who harvest gold, shear snow, or in casks store the crushed
purple, be it either religion or love, Galatea, though without
a shrine, is deity.

17

Not without altars: for the edge of the foaming sea, where
she checks her light foot, is an altar for the first fruits of the
laborer, for the shearings of the shepherd; the gardener
pours all the horn of plenty, hardly miserly toward the earth,
over the wicker which his honest daughter copiously, if not
artfully, wove.

18

Youth burns, and the plows comb the lands they furrowed
before, badly guided, when not dragged by slow oxen, er-
rant like their master; without a shepherd to whistle to them,
the flocks fail to recognize the resounding creaks of the slings,
unless instead of the poor shepherd Zephyrus whistles or the
oaktree creaks.

19

Silent at night the dog, asleep during the day, stretches from
hill to hill and shadow to shadow; the flock bleats; at the
forlorn bleating the wolf is born from the shadows: he gluts
himself, and savagely leaves moist with the blood of one,
that which another grazes upon. Love, renew the whistlings,
or let the silence of the dog, and sleep, follow its master.

20

La fugitiva Ninfa en tanto, donde
hurta un laurel su tronco al Sol ardiente,
tanto jazmines cuanta yerba esconde
la nieve de sus miembros da a una fuente.
Dulce se queja, dulce le responde
un ruiseñor a otro, y dulcemente
al sueño da sus ojos la armonía,
por no abrasar con tres soles el día.

21

Salamandria del Sol, vestido estrellas,
latiendo el can del cielo estaba, cuando,
polvo el cabello, húmidas centellas,
si no ardientes aljófares sudando,
llegó Acis, y de ambas luces bellas
dulce Occidente viendo al sueño blando,
su boca dió, y sus ojos, cuanto pudo,
a sonoro cristal, al cristal mudo.

22

Era Acis un venablo de Cupido,
de un Fauno, medio hombre medio fiera,
en Simetis, hermosa Ninfa, habido;
gloria del mar, honor de su ribera.
El bello imán, el ídolo dormido,
que acero sigue, idólatra venera,
rico de cuanto el huerto ofrece pobre,
rinden las vacas y fomenta el robre.

23

El celestial humor recién cuajado
que la almendra guardó, entre verde y seca,
en blanca mimbre se le puso al lado,
y un copo, en verdes juncos, de manteca;
en breve corcho, pero bien labrado,
un rubio hijo de una encina hueca,
dulcísimo panal, a cuya cera
su néctar vinculó la Primavera.

20

Meanwhile the fleeing nymph, where a laurel steals its trunk from the burning sun, gives the snow of her limbs (jasmines enough to hide the grass) to a fountain. Sweetly one nightingale laments, sweetly another answers, and sweetly the harmony gives her eyes to sleep, so that the day need not burn with three suns.

21

Salamander of the sun, clad in stars, the dog was barking from heaven, when, dust his hair, sweating humid sparks, if not burning pearls, Acis arrived, and seeing the sweet sunset of both lovely eyes to gentle sleep, he put his mouth to the sonorous crystal and his eyes, as much as he could, to the mute crystal.

22

Acis was a Cupid's arrow, begot by a faun, half man half beast, on Symaethis, lovely nymph; glory of the sea, honor of its shore. Rich in what the poor garden offers, in what the cows render, in what the oak produces, he idolatrously worships the beautiful magnet that steel follows, the sleeping idol.

23

He set by her side in a white basket the heavenly liquid, just curdled, which the almond, halfway between green and dry, stored, and a flake, in green reeds, of butter; in a small but well-fashioned flask of cork, the sweetest honeycomb (blond offspring of a hollow oak), to whose wax Spring linked its nectar.

24

Caluroso, al arroyo da las manos,
y con ellas, las ondas a su frente,
entre dos mirtos que, de espuma canos,
dos verdes garzas son de la corriente.
Vagas cortinas de volantes vanos
corrió Favonio lisonjeramente,
a la, del viento cuando no sea, cama
de frescas sombras, de menuda grama.

25

La Ninfa, pues, la sonorosa plata
bullir sintió del arroyuelo apenas,
cuando, a los verdes márgenes ingrata,
seguir se hizo de sus azucenas.
Huyera, mas tan frío se desata
un temor perezoso por sus venas,
que a la precisa fuga, al presto vuelo
grillos de nieve fué, plumas de hielo.

26

Fruta en mimbres halló, leche exprimida
en juncos, miel en corcho, mas sin dueño;
si bien al dueño debe, agradecida,
su deidad culta, venerado el sueño.
A la ausencia mil veces ofrecida,
este de cortesía no pequeño
indicio, la dejó, aunque estatua helada,
más discursiva y menos alterada.

27

No al Cíclope atribuye, no, la ofrenda;
no a Sátiro lascivo, ni a otro feo
morador de las selvas, cuya rienda
el sueño aflija que aflojó el deseo.
El niño dios, entonces, de la venda,
ostentación gloriosa, alto trofeo
quiere que al árbol de su madre sea
el desdén hasta allí de Galatea.

24

Hot, he gives his hands to the brook, and with them, the billows to his brow, between two myrtle bushes which, hoary with foam, are two green herons of the current. Favonius caressingly drew filmy curtains of thin fabric over the bed, if not of the wind, of cool shadows, of fine grass.

25

The nymph, then, faintly heard the sonorous silver of the rivulet effervesce, when, ungrateful to the green banks, she became a hatchet to their lilies. She would flee, but a lazy fear goes coursing through her veins so coldly that it was to immediate flight, to swift escape, manacles of snow, feathers of ice.

26

She found fruit in wicker, compressed milk in reeds, honey in cork, but without owner; although she thankfully owes to the owner her deity worshipped, her sleep venerated. A thousand times inured to absence, this no small sign of courtesy left her, frozen statue though she was, more discursive and less troubled.

27

Not to the Cyclops does she attribute the offering, no; not to the lascivious Satyr, nor to any other ugly denizen of the woods, whose reins, which desire weakened, may sleep afflict. The blindfold boy-god thereupon desires the present disdain of Galatea to be a glorious ostentation, a lofty trophy for his mother's tree.

28

Entre las ramas de el que más se lava
en el arroyo, mirto levantado,
carcaj de cristal hizo, si no aljaba,
su blando pecho de un arpón dorado.
El monstruo de rigor, la fiera brava,
mira la ofrenda ya con más cuidado,
y aun siente que a su dueño sea devoto,.
confuso alcaide más, el verde soto.

29

Llamárale, aunque muda; mas no sabe
el nombre articular que más querría,
ni le ha visto; si bien pincel süave
le ha bosquejado ya en su fantasía.
Al pie, no tanto ya del temor grave,
fía su intento; y, tímida, en la umbría
cama de campo y campo de batalla,
fingiendo sueño al cauto garzón halla.

30

El bulto vió, y haciéndole dormido,
librada en un pie toda sobre él pende,
urbana al sueño, bárbara al mentido
retórico silencio que no entiende:
no el ave reina así el fragoso nido
corona inmóvil, mientras no desciende,
rayo con plumas, al milano pollo,
que la eminencia abriga de un escollo,

31

como la Ninfa bella, compitiendo
con el garzón dormido en cortesía,
no sólo para, mas dulce estruendo
de el lento arroyo enmudecer querría.
A pesar luego de las ramas, viendo
colorido el bosquejo que ya había
en su imaginación Cupido hecho,
con el pincel que le clavó su pecho,

28

Among the branches of the upright myrtle, that which most
bathes in the stream, her soft breast made a quiver of crystal,
if not a holster, for a golden harpoon. The monster of se-
verity, the wild beast, now looks upon the offering with
greater care, and even feels that the green grove is sacred to
its owner, its perplexed warden rather.

29

She would call him, though mute; but she does not know
how to articulate the name she would love most, nor has
she seen him, and yet already in her fancy a gentle brush has
sketched him. No longer struck by so great a fear, she trusts
to her foot her intentions; and on the shady bed of field and
field of battle, she timidly comes upon the wary lad feigning
sleep.

30

She saw his form, and thinking him asleep, balanced on one
foot, she leans over him, urbane to sleep, barbarous to the
deceitful rhetorical silence she does not understand. The
queen bird, motionless, does not so crown the craggy nest,
when it is not descending, feathered lightning, upon the
kite's young which the jutting of a cliff shelters,

31

as the lovely nymph, competing in courtesy with the sleeping
lad, not only pauses, but would have the sweet clamor of
the slow brook become mute. Then, in spite of the branches,
seeing the sketch now colored that Cupid had already made
in her imagination, with the brush or arrow that pierced her
breast,

32

de sitio mejorada, atenta mira,
en la disposición robusta, aquello
que, si por lo süave no la admira,
es fuerza que la admire por lo bello.
De el casi tramontado Sol aspira,
a los confusos rayos, su cabello:
flores su bozo es, cuyas colores,
como duerme la luz, niegan las flores.

33

(En la rústica greña yace oculto
el áspid de el intonso prado ameno,
antes que de el peinado jardín culto
en el lascivo, regalado seno.)
En lo viril desata de su bulto
lo más dulce el Amor de su veneno:
bébelo Galatea, y da otro paso,
por apurarle la ponzoña al vaso.

34

Acis, aún más de aquello que dispensa
la brújula de el sueño vigilante,
alterada la Ninfa esté, o suspensa,
Argos es siempre atento a su semblante,
lince penetrador de lo que piensa,
cíñalo bronce o múrelo diamante;
que en sus Paladïones Amor ciego,
sin romper muros, introduce fuego.

35

El sueño de sus miembros sacudido,
gallardo el joven la persona ostenta,
y al marfil luego de sus pies rendido,
el coturno besar dorado intenta.
Menos ofende el rayo prevenido
al marinero, menos la tormenta
prevista le turbó, o prognosticada:
Galatea lo diga salteada.

32

having bettered her position, she looks intently at that, in his
robust lineaments, which, if for its softness she did not admire
it, she would be forced to admire for its beauty. His hair
aspires to the confused rays of the almost set sun: the down
on his lips is flowers whose colors, when the light sleeps, are
denied by the flowers.

33

In the rustic elflocks of the pleasant unshorn meadow the
asp lies hidden, rather than in the lascivious, delightful
bosom of the well-combed cultivated garden. In the virility
of his form Love releases the sweetest essence of his venom.
Galatea drinks it, and takes another step to drain the poison
from the vessel.

34

Acis, even more than that which the peephole of vigilant
sleep concedes, whether the nymph be troubled or hesitant,
is always Argus fixed upon her countenance, penetrating lynx
of what she is thinking, though she gird it with bronze or wall
it with diamond; for into her Palladia blind Love, without
breaking through walls, introduces fire.

35

Sleep shaken from his limbs, the youth gracefully displays
himself, and surrendering then to the ivory of her feet,
undertakes to kiss the golden slipper. Less the expected
lightning harms the sailor, less the storm, foreseen or pre-
dicted, unsettled her: may Galatea say so, taken by surprise.

36

Más agradable, y menos zahareña,
al mancebo levanta venturoso,
dulce ya concediéndole, y risueña,
paces no al sueño, treguas sí al reposo.
Lo cóncavo hacía de una peña
a un fresco sitïal dosel umbroso,
y verdes celosías unas yedras,
trepando troncos y abrazando piedras.

37

Sobre una alfombra, que imitara en vano
el tirio sus matices, si bien era
de cuantas sedas ya hiló gusano
y artífiçe tejió la Primavera,
reclinados, al mirto más lozano
una y otra lasciva, si ligera,
paloma se caló, cuyos gemidos,
trompas de Amor, alteran sus oídos.

38

El ronco arrullo al joven solicita;
mas, con desvíos Galatea süaves,
a su audacia los términos limita,
y el aplauso al concento de las aves.
Entre las ondas y la fruta, imita
Acis al siempre ayuno en penas graves:
que, en tanta gloria, infierno son no breve
fugitivo cristal, pomos de nieve.

39

No a las palomas concedió Cupido
juntar de sus dos picos los rubíes,
cuando al clavel el joven atrevido
las dos hojas le chupa carmesíes.
Cuantas produce Pafo, engendra Gnido,
negras vïolas, blancos alhelíes,
llueven sobre el que Amor quiere que sea
tálamo de Acis y de Galatea.

36

More amiable and less haughty, she sweetly and smilingly
raises up the lucky lad, not conceding peace to sleep, rather
truce to rest. The hollowness of a cliff made for a cool seat
a shady canopy, and some ivy-vines, climbing trunks and
embracing rocks, made green blinds.

37

As they lay reclining upon a carpet, whose tints in vain the
Tyrian dye would imitate, although it was of as many silks as
the worm had already spun or Spring had skilfully woven, on
the most luxuriant myrtle one and then another lascivious,
if bouyant dove alighted, whose sighs, trumpets of Love,
trouble their ears.

38

The deep-throated cooing arouses the youth; but with gentle
dodges Galatea marks boundaries to his boldness, and approval of the harmony of the birds. Between waves and fruit
Acis imitates him who is always fasting in great torment: for,
in such splendor, fleeing crystal, apples of snow, are a not
brief inferno.

39

Hardly had Cupid allowed the doves to join the rubies of
their two bills, when the emboldened youth sucks the two
crimson leaves of the carnation. May all the black violets,
white gilliflowers that Paphos produces, Cnidos engenders,
rain down upon what Love desires to be the bridal couch of
Acis and of Galatea.

40

Su aliento humo, sus relinchos fuego,
si bien su freno espumas, ilustraba
las columnas Etón, que erigió el Griego,
do el carro de la luz sus ruedas lava,
cuando, de Amor el fiero jayán ciego,
la cerviz oprimió a una roca brava,
que a la playa, de escollos no desnuda,
linterna es ciega y atalaya muda.

41

Árbitro de montañas y ribera,
aliento dió, en la cumbre de la roca,
a los albogues que agregó la cera,
el prodigioso fuelle de su boca;
la Ninfa los oyó, y ser más quisiera
breve flor, yerba humilde y tierra poca,
que de su nuevo tronco vid lasciva,
muerta de amor y de temor no viva.

42

Mas, cristalinos pámpanos sus brazos,
amor la implica, si el temor la anuda,
al infelice olmo, que pedazos
la segur de los celos hará, aguda.
Las cavernas en tanto, los ribazos
que ha prevenido la zampoña ruda,
el trueno de la voz fulminó luego:
referidlo, Piérides, os ruego.

43

"¡Oh, bella Galatea, más süave
que los claveles que tronchó la Aurora;
blanca más que las plumas de aquel ave
que dulce muere y en las aguas mora;
igual en pompa al pájaro que, grave,
su manto azul de tantos ojos dora
cuantas el celestial zafiro estrellas!
¡Oh tú que en dos incluyes las más bellas!

40

Its breath smoke, its neighing fire, though its bridle foam,
Ethon illuminated the pillars that the Greek erected, where
the chariot of light laves its wheels, when, blind with love
the fierce giant crushed the neck of a stalwart cliff, which
for the shore, not barren of shoals, is a blind beacon and a
silent watchtower.

41

Arbiter of mountains and shore, on the summit of the cliff
the prodigious bellows of his mouth gave breath to the reeds
that the wax joined; the nymph heard them and would rather
be a small flower, humble plant, and little earth, than the
sportive vine of his new trunk, dead she was of love and
lifeless with fear.

42

But (her arms crystal vineshoots) love binds her, while fear
ties her to the unhappy elm which the sharp axe of jealousy
will cut to pieces. Meanwhile the thunder of the voice then
struck the caves, the hills which the rude pipes had forewarned: set it forth, Pierides, I beg you.

43

"O lovely Galatea, softer than the carnations the Dawn
reaped; whiter than the plumes of that bird that sweetly dies
and dwells in the water; equal in splendor to the bird that
sedately gilds its blue mantel with as many eyes as the
celestial sapphire with stars! O you who in two of them
comprise the most beautiful!

44

"Deja las ondas, deja el rubio coro
de las hijas de Tetis, y el mar vea,
cuando niega la luz un carro de oro,
que en dos la restituye Galatea.
Pisa la arena, que en la arena adoro
cuantas el blanco pie conchas platea,
cuyo bello contacto puede hacerlas,
sin concebir rocío, parir perlas.

45

"Sorda hija de el mar, cuyas orejas
a mis gemidos son rocas al viento;
o dormida te hurten a mis quejas
purpúreos troncos de corales ciento,
o al disonante número de almejas,
marino, si agradable no, instrumento,
coros tejiendo estés, escucha un día
mi voz, por dulce cuando no por mía.

46

"Pastor soy, mas tan rico de ganados
que los valles impido más vacíos,
los cerros desparezco levantados,
y los caudales seco de los ríos:
no los que, de sus ubres desatados
o derribados de los ojos míos,
leche corren y lágrimas; que iguales
en número a mis bienes son mis males.

47

"Sudando néctar, lambicando olores,
senos que ignora aún la golosa cabra
corchos me guardan, más que abeja flores
liba inquïeta, ingenïosa labra;
troncos me ofrecen árboles mayores,
cuyos enjambres, o el abril los abra
o los desate el mayo, ámbar destilan,
y en ruecas de oro rayos de el Sol hilan.

44

Leave the waves, leave the blond chorus of Thetis' daughters, let the ocean see that when a golden chariot withdraws the light Galatea doubly restores it. Walk upon the sand, for on the sand I worship all the shells your white foot silvers, whose lovely touch can make them, without conceiving dew, bear pearls.

45

Deaf child of the ocean, whose ears to my sighs are rocks to the wind; whether the purple stalks of a hundred corals steal thee sleeping from my laments, or whether to the dissonant measure of clams (marine, if unpleasing, instrument) you may be weaving dances, listen some day to my voice, for its being sweet if not for its being mine.

46

I am a shepherd; but so rich in flocks that I obstruct the emptiest valleys, level the exalted hills, dry up the floods of the rivers: not those that, freed from their udders or derived from my eyes, run milk and tears; for equal in number to my goods are my misfortunes.

47

Cork keeps for me repositories sweating nectar, distilling odors, which even the greedy goat misses, more than the flowers that the bee sucks restlessly and ingeniously transforms; the largest trees offer me their trunks, whose swarms, whether April open or May loosen them, distill amber and spin sunbeams on distaffs of gold.

48

"De el Júpiter soy hijo de las ondas,
aunque pastor; si tu desdén no espera
a que el Monarca de esas grutas hondas
en trono de cristal te abrace nuera;
Polifemo te llama, no te escondas
que tanto esposo admira la ribera,
cual otro no vió Febo más robusto,
del perezoso Volga al Indo adusto.

49

"Sentado, a la alta palma no perdona
su dulce fruto mi robusta mano,
en pie, sombra capaz es mi persona
de innumerables cabras el verano.
¿Qué mucho si de nubes se corona
por igualarme la montaña en vano,
y en los cielos, desde esta roca, puedo
escribir mis desdichas con el dedo?

50

"Marítimo Alcïón, roca eminente
sobre sus huevos coronaba, el día
que espejo de zafiro fué luciente
la playa azul de la persona mía;
miréme, y lucir vi un sol en mi frente,
cuando en el cielo un ojo se veía:
neutra el agua dudaba a cuál fe preste:
o al cielo humano o al Cíclope celeste.

51

"Registra en otras puertas el venado
sus años, su cabeza colmilluda
la fiera, cuyo cerro levantado
de Helvecias picas es muralla aguda;
la humana suya el caminante errado
dió ya a mi cueva, de piedad desnuda,
albergue hoy por tu causa al peregrino,
do halló reparo, si perdió camino.

48

I am the son of the Jupiter of the waves, though a shepherd, even if your disdain does not expect the monarch of those deep grottoes on his throne of crystal to embrace you as his daughter-in-law; Polyphemus calls you; do not hide yourself, for the shore marvels at such a husband as Phoebus never saw another more robust, from the lazy Volga to the parched Indus.

49

When I sit my robust hand does not pardon the tall palm its sweet fruit; when I stand my body is a capacious shadow, in summer, for innumerable goats. What wonder if in vain to equal me the mountain crowns itself with clouds, and in the heavens from this cliff I can write my misfortunes with my finger?

50

Sea-going Alcyon, upon its eggs, crowned the jutting cliff, the day the blue beach was a lucent sapphire mirror of my person; I looked at myself and saw a sun gleam in my forehead, while in the sky an eye was seen: the neutral water doubted in which it should trust, in the human sky or in the skyey Cyclops.

51

On other doors the stag records its years, the wild beast whose reared back is a sharp wall of Helvetian pikes records its fanged head; the lost traveler once gave his human head to my cave, naked of pity, today a lodging for the stranger, where, for your sake, he found succour if he lost his way.

52
"En tablas dividida, rica nave
besó la playa miserablemente,
de cuantas vomitó riquezas grave,
por las bocas de el Nilo el Orïente.
Yugo aquel día, y yugo bien süave,
de el fiero mar a la sañuda frente,
imponiéndole estaba, si no al viento,
dulcísimas coyundas mi instrumento;

53
"Cuando, entre globos de agua, entregar veo
a las arenas ligurina haya,
en cajas los aromas de el Sabeo,
en cofres las riquezas de Cambaya;
delicias de aquel mundo, ya trofeo
de Scila que, ostentado en nuestra playa,
lastimoso despojo fué dos días
a las que esta montaña engendra harpías.

54
"Segunda tabla a un Ginovés mi gruta
de su persona fué, de su hacienda:
la una reparada, la otra enjuta.
Relación de el naufragio hizo horrenda.
Luciente paga de la mejor fruta
que en yerbas se recline, en hilos penda,
colmillo fué de el animal que el Ganges
sufrir muros le vió, romper falanges.

55
"Arco, digo, gentil, bruñida aljaba,
obras ambas de artífice prolijo,
y de malaco rey a deidad java
alto don, según ya mi huésped dijo.
De aquél la mano, de ésta el hombro agrava:
convencida la madre, imita al hijo:
serás a un tiempo, en estos horizontes,
Venus de el mar, Cupido de los montes."

52

Split into planks, a ship wretchedly kissed the beach, rich
in all the riches the heavy Orient spewed forth from the
mouths of the Nile. A yoke that day and a yoke quite mild,
my instrument was forcing upon the wrathful brow of the
wild sea, if not upon the wind, the gentlest halters;

53

when, between globes of water, I see the Ligurian beechtree
deliver to the sands in boxes the fragrances of the Sheban,
in chests the riches of Cambay; delights of that world, now
Scylla's trophy, which, displayed upon our beach, was for
two days the lamentable spoils of the Harpies this mountain
engenders.

54

For a Genoese my grotto was a second plank to his body, to
his fortune: the one was sheltered, the other dried. A fearful
account of his shipwreck he gave. Gleaming reward for the
best fruit that lies upon the grass, hangs in threads, was the
tusk of the animal which the Ganges saw bear walls, break
phalanxes.

55

A noble bow, I add, a burnished quiver, both works of a
copious artisan, lofty gift of Moluccan king to Javanese god-
dess, as my guest said. With the one encumber your hand,
with the other your shoulder: once the mother is won over,
imitate the son: on these horizons you shall be at one and the
same time Venus of the sea, Cupid of the mountains."

56
Su horrenda voz, no su dolor interno,
cabras aquí le interrumpieron, cuantas,
vagas el pie, sacrílegas el cuerno,
a Baco se atrevieron en sus plantas.
Mas, conculcado el pámpano más tierno
viendo el fiero pastor, voces él tantas,
y tantas despidió la honda piedras,
que el muro penetraron de las yedras.

57
De los nudos, con esto, más süaves,
los dulces dos amantes desatados,
por duras guijas, por espinas graves
solicitan el mar con pies alados:
tal redimiendo de importunas aves
incauto meseguero sus sembrados,
de liebres dirimió copia así amiga,
que vario sexo unió y un surco abriga.

58
Viendo el fiero jayán con paso mudo
correr al mar la fugitiva nieve,
que a tanta vista el Líbico desnudo
registra el campo de su adarga breve,
y al garzón viendo, cuantas mover pudo
celoso trueno, antiguas hayas mueve:
tal, antes que la opaca nube rompa
previene rayo fulminante trompa.

59
Con vïolencia desgajó, infinita,
la mayor punta de la excelsa roca,
que al joven, sobre quien la precipita,
urna es mucha, pirámide no poca.
Con lágrimas la Ninfa solicita
las Deidades de el mar, que Acis invoca:
concurren todas, y el peñasco duro,
la sangre que exprimió, cristal fué puro.

56

His fearful voice, not his inner pain, goats here interrupted, all that dared, wandering of foot, sacrilegious of horn, upon the vines of Bacchus. But the fierce shepherd, seeing the tenderest vineshoot trampled, despatched so many shrieks, and his sling so many stones, that they penetrated the wall of ivy.

57

The two sweet lovers, unloosened at this from the most pleasing bonds, over hard pebbles, over harsh thorns, seek the ocean with winged feet: like a reckless harvest-watcher who, in redeeming his seed-beds from importunate birds, thus scattered a friendly abundance of hares which differing sex united and a furrow shelters.

58

The fierce giant, seeing the fugitive snow with silent step running toward the sea (for with such distant vision the naked Libyan makes out the expanse of their small shields) and, seeing the youth, moves all the ancient beechtrees jealous thunder could move: so, before the opaque cloud divides, thunder proclaims the flashing trumpet.

59

With infinite violence he tore loose the greatest peak of the lofty cliff, which for the youth, over whom he dashes it, is an ample urn, a not-scanty pyramid. With tears the nymph entreats the deities of the sea, whom Acis calls upon: all gather; and the blood that the heavy boulder pressed out was pure crystal.

60

Sus miembros lastimosamente opresos
del escollo fatal fueron apenas,
que los pies de los árboles más gruesos
calzó el líquido aljófar de sus venas.
Corriendo plata al fin sus blancos huesos,
lamiendo flores y argentando arenas,
a Doris llega, que con llanto pío,
yerno le saludó, le aclamó río.

60

Hardly had his limbs been lamentably crushed by the deadly rock than the liquid pearl of his veins covered the feet of the stoutest trees. Finally, his white bones running argent, licking flowers and silvering sands, he reaches Doris, who with merciful lament greeted him as a son-in-law, acclaimed him as a river.

NOTE: *My English version of the "Polifemo" is offered as an aid to understanding a difficult poem. Several cruxes have been boldly rendered according to my present views, though many alternate interpretations would seem possible. All along, my aim has been to translate as literally as possible within the bound of intelligibility. For commentary see Bernardo Alemany y Selfa,* Vocabulario de las obras de Góngora *(Madrid, 1930) and Antonio Vilanova,* Las fuentes y los temas del Polifemo de Góngora, *2 vols. (Madrid, 1957). The latter, oppressively exhaustive, has the virtue of quoting the early commentators, José Pellicer (1630) and García de Salcedo Coronel (1636).*

John Milton: "Lycidas"

Yet once more, O ye Laurels, and once more
Ye Myrtles brown, with Ivy never sere,
I come to pluck your Berries harsh and crude,
And with forc'd fingers rude,
Shatter your leaves before the mellowing year.
Bitter constraint, and sad occasion dear,
Compels me to disturb your season due:
For *Lycidas* is dead, dead ere his prime,
Young *Lycidas,* and hath not left his peer:
Who would not sing for *Lycidas?* he knew   10
Himself to sing, and build the lofty rhyme.
He must not float upon his wat'ry bier
Unwept, and welter to the parching wind,
Without the meed of some melodious tear.
   Begin then, Sisters of the sacred well,
That from beneath the seat of *Jove* doth spring,
Begin, and somewhat loudly sweep the string.
Hence with denial vain, and coy excuse,
So may some gentle Muse
With lucky words favour my destin'd Urn,   20
And as he passes turn,
And bid fair peace be to my sable shroud.
For we were nurst upon the self-same hill,
Fed the same flock, by fountain, shade, and rill.
   Together both, ere the high Lawns appear'd

Under the opening eye-lids of the morn,
We drove afield, and both together heard
What time the Gray-fly winds her sultry horn,
Batt'ning our flocks with the fresh dews of night,
Oft till the Star that rose, at Ev'ning, bright   30
Toward Heav'n's descent had slop'd his westering wheel.
Meanwhile the Rural ditties were not mute,
Temper'd to th'Oaten Flute;
Rough *Satyrs* danc'd, and *Fauns* with clov'n heel,
From the glad sound would not be absent long,
    nd old *Damaetas* lov'd to hear our song.
    But O the heavy change, now thou art gone,
Now thou art gone, and never must return!
Thee Shepherd, thee the Woods, and desert Caves,
With wild Thyme and the gadding Vine o'ergrown,   40
And all their echoes mourn.
The Willows and the Hazel Copses green
Shall now no more be seen,
Fanning their joyous Leaves to thy soft lays.
As killing as the Canker to the Rose,
Or Taint-worm to the weanling Herds that graze,
Or Frost to Flowers, that their gay wardrobe wear,
When first the White-thorn blows,
Such, *Lycidas*, thy loss to Shepherd's ear.
    Where were ye Nymphs when the remorseless deep   50
Clos'd o'er the head of your lov'd *Lycidas?*
For neither were ye playing on the steep,
Where your old *Bards,* the famous *Druids,* lie,
Nor on the shaggy top of *Mona* high,
Nor yet where *Deva* spreads her wizard stream:
Ay me, I fondly dream!
Had ye been there—for what could that have done?
What could the Muse herself that *Orpheus* bore,
The Muse herself, for her enchanting son
Whom Universal nature did lament,   60
When by the rout that made the hideous roar,

His gory visage down the stream was sent,
Down the swift *Hebrus* to the *Lesbian* shore?
   Alas! What boots it with uncessant care
To tend the homely slighted Shepherd's trade,
And strictly meditate the thankless Muse?
Were it not better done as others use,
To sport with *Amaryllis* in the shade,
Or with the tangles of *Neaera's* hair?
Fame is the spur that the clear spirit doth raise   70
(That last infirmity of Noble mind)
To scorn delights, and live laborious days;
But the fair Guerdon when we hope to find,
And think to burst out into sudden blaze,
Comes the blind *Fury* with th'abhorred shears,
And slits the thin-spun life. But not the praise,
Phoebus repli'd, and touch'd my trembling ears;
Fame is no plant that grows on mortal soil,
Nor in the glistering foil
Set off to th'world, nor in broad rumour lies,   80
But lives and spreads aloft by those pure eyes
And perfect witness of all judging *Jove;*
As he pronounces lastly on each deed,
Of so much fame in Heav'n expect thy meed.
   O Fountain Arethuse, and thou honour'd flood,
Smooth-sliding *Mincius,* crown'd with vocal reeds,
That strain I heard was of a higher mood:
But now my Oat proceeds,
And listens to the Herald of the Sea
That came in *Neptune's* plea.   90
He ask'd the Waves, and ask'd the Felon winds,
What hard mishap hath doom'd this gentle swain?
And question'd every gust of rugged wings
That blows from off each beaked Promontory.
They knew not of his story,
And sage Hippotades their answer brings,
That not a blast was from his dungeon stray'd,

The Air was calm, and on the level brine,
Sleek *Panope* with all her sisters play'd.
It was that fatal and perfidious Bark 100
Built in th'eclipse, and rigg'd with curses dark,
That sunk so low that sacred head of thine.
 Next *Camus*, reverend Sire, went footing slow,
His Mantle hairy, and his Bonnet sedge,
Inwrought with figures dim, and on the edge
Like to that sanguine flower inscrib'd with woe.
Ah! Who hath reft (quoth he) my dearest pledge?
Last came, and last did go,
The Pilot of the *Galilean* lake.
Two massy Keys he bore of metals twain, 110
(The Golden opes, the Iron shuts amain).
He shook his Mitred locks, and stern bespake:
How well could I have spar'd for thee, young swain,
Enough of such as for their bellies' sake,
Creep and intrude and climb into the fold?
Of other care they little reck'ning make,
Than how to scramble at the shearers' feast,
And shove away the worthy bidden guest.
Blind mouths! that scarce themselves know how to hold
A Sheep-hook, or have learn'd aught else the least 120
That to the faithful Herdman's art belongs!
What recks it them? What need they? They are sped;
And when they list, their lean and flashy songs
Grate on their scrannel Pipes of wretched straw.
The hungry Sheep look up, and are not fed,
But swoln with wind, and the rank mist they draw,
Rot inwardly, and foul contagion spread:
Besides what the grim Wolf with privy paw
Daily devours apace, and nothing said;
But that two-handed engine at the door 130
Stands ready to smite once, and smite no more.
 Return *Alpheus*, the dread voice is past,
That shrunk thy streams; Return *Sicilian* Muse,

And call the Vales, and bid them hither cast
Their Bells and Flowrets of a thousand hues.
Ye valleys low where the mild whispers use
Of shades and wanton winds and gushing brooks,
On whose fresh lap the swart Star sparely looks,
Throw hither all your quaint enamell'd eyes,
That on the green turf suck the honied showers,   140
And purple all the ground with vernal flowers.
Bring the rathe Primrose that forsaken dies,
The tufted Crow-toe, and pale Jessamine,
The white Pink, and the Pansy freakt with jet,
The glowing Violet,
The Musk-rose, and the well attir'd Woodbine,
With Cowslips wan that hang the pensive head,
And every flower that sad embroidery wears:
Bid *Amaranthus* all his beauty shed,
And Daffadillies fill their cups with tears,   150
To strew the Laureate Hearse where *Lycid* lies.
For so to interpose a little ease,
Let our frail thoughts dally with false surmise.
Ay me! Whilst thee the shores, and sounding Seas
Wash far away, where'er thy bones are hurl'd,
Whether beyond the stormy *Hebrides,*
Where thou perhaps under the whelming tide
Visit'st the bottom of the monstrous world;
Or whether thou to our moist vows denied,
Sleep'st by the fable of *Bellerus* old,   160
Where the great vision of the guarded Mount
Looks toward *Namancos* and *Bayona's* hold;
Look homeward Angel now, and melt with ruth:
And, O ye *Dolphins,* waft the hapless youth.
   Weep no more, woeful Shepherds weep no more,
For *Lycidas* your sorrow is not dead,
Sunk though he be beneath the wat'ry floor,
So sinks the day-star in the Ocean bed,
And yet anon repairs his drooping head,

And tricks his beams, and with new spangled Ore,   170
Flames in the forehead of the morning sky:
So *Lycidas,* sunk low, but mounted high,
Through the dear might of him that walk'd the waves,
Where other groves, and other streams along,
With *Nectar* pure his oozy Locks he laves
And hears the unexpressive nuptial Song,
In the blest Kingdoms meek of joy and love.
There entertain him all the Saints above,
In solemn troops, and sweet Societies
That sing, and singing in their glory move,   180
And wipe the tears for ever from his eyes.
Now *Lycidas* the Shepherds weep no more;
Henceforth thou art the Genius of the shore,
In thy large recompense, and shalt be good
To all that wander in that perilous flood.

   Thus sang the uncouth Swain to th'Oaks and rills,
While the still morn went out with Sandals gray.
He touch't the tender stops of various Quills,
With eager thought warbling his *Doric* lay:
And now the sun had stretch't out all the hills,   190
And now was dropt into the Western bay;
At last he rose, and twitch't his Mantle blue:
Tomorrow to fresh Woods, and Pastures new.

Giambattista Marino: "Amori notturni"

Quando, stanco dal corso, a Teti in seno
per trovar posa e pace,
Febo si corca e 'l dì ne fura e cela,
e nel tranquillo mar, nel ciel sereno
ogni euro, ogni aura tace,
dorme il marino armento e l'onda gela;
allor ch'emula al giorno,
Notte, spiegando intorno
il suo manto gemmato, il mondo vela,
e tant'occhi apre il ciel, quanti ne serra,   10
vaghi di sonno e di riposo, in terra;
 allor Lilla gentil, l'anima mia,
da la gelosa madre
e dal ritroso genitor s'invola:
indi, per chiusa e solitaria via,
di vaghe orme leggiadre
stampa l'arena, e, taciturna e sola
(se non quanto va seco
Amor per l'aer cieco),
mentre pesce non guizza, augel non vola,   20
rinchiusa in un beato antro m'attende,
antro che da le Fate il nome prende.
 Io, cui lunge da lei grave è la vita,
tosto che 'l ciel s'imbruna,
sconosciuto colà drizzo le piante.

Quasi notturno sol, la via m'addita,
nuda e senz'ombra alcuna,
Cinzia, qual pria s'offerse al caro amante,
e già ferir la miro
da l'argentato giro   30
di ceruleo splendor l'onda tremante;
e, fatte a mio favor più che mai belle,
spettatrici d'amor veggio le stelle.
    Giunto al mio ben, chi potria dir gli spessi,
i lunghi, i molli baci?
i sospir tronchi? i languidi lamenti?
Chi può contar degli amorosi amplessi
le catene tenaci?
gli accesi squardi? gl'interrotti accenti?
gli atti dolci e furtivi?   40
gli atti dolci e lascivi?
Tanti sono i diletti, e sì possenti,
che dal cor per se stessa si divide
l'anima, e innanzi tempo amor m'uccide.
    Lentando allor, ma non sciogliendo il laccio,
con la prima dolcezza
temprato alquanto il fervido desio,
languidamente l'un a l'altro in braccio,
vinti da la stanchezza,
ce ne stiam vaneggiando, ed ella ed io.   50
Mentre pian pian col manco
a lei stringo il bel fianco,
e con l'altro altra parte ascosa spio,
ella d'ambe le sue, peso non grave,
fa quasi al collo mio giogo soave.
    Io narro a lei, favoleggiando intanto,
quando primier mi prese,
e l'ora e 'l punto e la maniera e 'l loco:
poi dico:—E da quel dì ch'amor cotanto
degli occhi tuoi m'accese,   60
sprezzai (sì dolce n'arsi) ogni altro foco.

Questi il mio 'ncendio fûro,
e per questi ti giuro
che d'ogni altra bellezza mi cal poco.
Clorida il ti può dir, d'Ergasto figlia,
quantunque ella sia bruna e tu vermiglia.
    Questa ognor mi lusinga e prega e chiama,
ma tutto indarno. . .—Allora
mi risponde colei ch'io stringo e suggo:
—Caro Fileno, e tu non sai se m'ama   70
e mi segue e m'adora
Tirinto il biondo, se io l'aborro e fuggo?
Quanti doni mi porge,
misero! e non s'accorge
ch'io per te sola. . .—e vuol seguir:—. . .mi struggo—;
ma, mosso dal piacer che 'l cor mi tocca,
le chiudo allor la sua con la mia bocca.
    Qui risorto il desio, qual d'arco strale,
ver' l'ultimo diletto
sen corre a sciolto fren, carco d'ardore.   80
Tra noi scherzando e dibattendo l'ale,
l'ignudo pargoletto
fa traboccar d'estrema gioia il core.
Su l'arena a cadere
n'andiam: con qual piacere,
questo mi tacerò, dicalo Amore;
anzi faccial per prova altrui sentire,
ché forse anch'egli Amor nol sapria dire.
    Stanco, non sazio, alfine alzo a' begli occhi
gli occhi tremanti, e poi   90
da le sue labra il fior de l'alma coglio;
e, mentre il molle seno avien ch'io tocchi,
e vo tra' pomi suoi
scherzando, e mille baci or dono or toglio,
tal, che lasso pareva,
pronto si desta e leva,
ond'io pur di morir dolce m'invoglio;

ma là dove più ingordo altri si sforza,
per soverchio desir manca la forza.
  Così mi giaccio, inutil pondo, appresso   100
a la mia ninfa amata,
ch'irride il mio stupor rigido e strano.
Per ch'io m'adiro e dico:—O di me stesso
parte vile insensata,
chi fia più che t'avivi, oimè!, se 'nvano
sì vezzosa ed amica
più volte s'affatica
di farti risentir la bella mano?
Certo di sasso sei, ma come, ahi lasso!
come sì molle sei, se sei di sasso?—   110
  Ed ecco uscir fuor de le rive estreme
de l'indica pendice
rapido il sol, da la sua nunzia scorto.
Ella, ch'esser veduta ha scorno e teme,
sospirando mi dice:
—A Dio, ben rivedrenne, e fia di corto:
a che tanto affannarte?—
Poi mi bacia e si parte.
Io resto e dico:—Invan per me se' sorto,
invido sol, ché questa notte oscura   120
era a me più che 'l dì lucida e pura!—
  Canzon, notturna sei,
notturni i furti miei:
non uscir, prego, al sol, fuggi la luce:
oblio più tosto eterno, ombra profonda
le mie vergogne e i tuoi difetti asconda.

Théophile de Viau: "La Solitude"

1

Dans ce val solitaire et sombre,
Le cerf qui brame au bruict de l'eau,
Panchant ses yeux dans un ruisseau,
S'amuse à regarder son ombre.

2

De ceste source une Naïade,
Tous les soirs ouvre le portail
De sa demeure de crystal,
Et nous chante une serenade.

3

Les Nymphes que la chasse attire
A l'ombrage de ces forests,
Cherchent des cabinets secrets,
Loing de l'embuche du Satire.

4

Jadis au pied de ce grand chesne,
Presque aussi vieux que le Soleil,
Bacchus, l'Amour et le Sommeil,
Feirent la fosse de Silene.

5

Un froid et tenebreux silence,
Dort à l'ombre de ses ormeaux,
Et les vents battent les rameaux
D'une amoureuse violence.

6

L'esprit plus retenu s'engage
Au plaisir de ce doux sejour,
Où Philomele nuict et jour,
Renouvelle un piteux langage.

7

L'orfraye et le hibou s'y perche,
Icy vivent les loups-garoux,
Jamais la justice en courroux
Icy de criminels ne cherche.

8

Icy l'amour faict ses Estudes,
Venus y dresse des autels,
Et les visites des mortels
Ne troublent point ces solitudes.

9

Ceste forest n'est point profane,
Ce ne fut point sans la fascher,
Qu'Amour y vint jadis cacher
Le berger qu'enseignoit Diane.

10

Amour pouvoit par innocence,
Comme enfant, tendre icy des retz,
Et comme Royne des forests,
Diane avoit ceste licence.

11

Cupidon d'une douce flamme
Ouvrant la nuict de ce valon,
Mist devant les yeux d'Apollon
Le garçon qu'il avoit dans l'ame.

12

A l'ombrage de ce bois sombre
Hyacinthe se retira:

Et depuis le Soleil jura,
Qu'il seroit ennemy de l'ombre.

13

Tout aupres le jaloux Boree,
Pressé d'un amoureux tourment,
Fut la mort de ce jeune amant
Encore par luy souspiree.

14

Saincte forest ma confidente,
Je jure par le Dieu du jour,
Que je n'auray jamais amour,
Que ne te soit toute evidente.

15

Mon Ange ira par cest ombrage,
Le Soleil le voyant venir,
Ressentira du souvenir
L'accez de sa premiere rage.

16

Corine je te prie approche,
Couchons nous sur ce tapis vert:
Et pour estre mieux à couvert,
Entrons au creux de ceste roche.

17

Ouvre tes yeux je te supplie,
Mille amours logent là dedans,
Et de leurs petits traits ardans
Ta prunelle est toute remplie:

18

Amour de tes regards souspire,
Et ton esclave devenu,
Se voit luy-mesme retenu
Dans les liens de son empire.

19

O beauté sans doute immortelle,
Où les Dieux trouvent des appas,
Par vos yeux je ne croyois pas
Que vous fussiez du tout si belle.

20

Qui voudroit faire une peinture,
Qui peust ses traits representer,
Il faudroit bien mieux inventer,
Que ne fera jamais nature.

21

Tout un siecle les destinees
Travaillerent apres ses yeux,
Et je croy que pour faire mieux
Le temps n'a point assez d'annees.

22

D'une fierté pleine d'amorce,
Ce beau visage a de regards,
Qui jettent des feux et des dards,
Dont les Dieux aymeroient la force.

23

Que ton teinct est de bonne grace!
Qu'il est blanc et qu'il est vermeil!
Il est plus net que le Soleil,
Et plus uni que de la glace.

24

Mon Dieu que tes cheveux me plaisent,
Ils s'esbattent dessus ton front,
Et les voyant beaux comme ils sont
Je suis jaloux quand ils te baisent.

25

Belle bouche d'ambre et de rose,
Ton entretien est desplaisant,

Si tu ne dis en me baisant,
Qu'aymer est une belle chose.

26

D'un air plein d'amoureuse flame,
Aux accens de ta douce voix,
Je voy les fleuves et les bois
S'embraser comme a faict mon ame.

27

Si tu moüilles tes doits d'yvoire
Dans le crystal de ce ruisseau,
Le Dieu qui loge dans ceste eau,
Aymera s'il en ose boire.

28

Presente luy ta face nuë
Tes yeux avecques l'eau riront,
Et dans ce miroir escriront
Que Venus est icy venuë.

29

Si bien elle y sera depeincte,
Les Faunes s'en enflammeront,
Et de tes yeux qu'ils aymeront
Ne sçauront descouvrir la feinte.

30

Entends ce Dieu qui te convie
A passer dans son Element,
Oy qu'il souspire bellement
Sa liberté desjà ravie.

31

Trouble luy ceste fantasie,
Destourne toy de ce miroir,
Tu le mettras au desespoir,
Et m'osteras la jalousie.

32

Voys-tu ce tronc et ceste pierre?
Je croy qu'ils prennent garde à nous,
Et mon amour devient jaloux
De ce myrthe et de ce lierre.

33

Sus ma Corine que je cueille
Tes baisers du matin au soir,
Voy comment pour nous faire asseoir
Ce myrthe a laissé choir sa fueille.

34

Oy le Pinçon et la Linotte,
Sur la branche de ce rosier,
Vois branler leur petit gosier,
Oy comme ils ont changé de notte.

35

Approche, approche ma Driade,
Icy murmureront les eaux,
Icy les amoureux oiseaux
Chanteront une serenade.

36

Preste moy ton sein pour y boire
Des odeurs qui m'embasmeront,
Ainsi mes sens se pasmeront
Dans les lacs de tes bras d'yvoire.

37

Je baigneray mes mains folastres
Dans les ondes de tes cheveux,
Et ta beauté prendra les voeux
De mes oeillades idolatres.

38

Ne crains rien, Cupidon nous garde,
Mon petit Ange es tu pas mien?

Ha! je voy que tu m'aymes bien,
Tu rougis quand je te regarde.

39

Dieux que ceste façon timide
Est puissante sur mes esprits!
Regnauld ne fut pas mieux espris
Par les charmes de son Armide.

40

Ma Corine que je t'embrasse,
Personne ne nous voit qu'Amor:
Voy que mesme les yeux du jour
Ne trouvent point icy de place.

41

Les vents qui ne se peuvent taire,
Ne peuvent escouter aussi,
Et ce que nous ferons icy
Leur est un incogneu mystere.

John Donne: "Loves Growth"

I Scarce beleeve my love to be so pure
   As I had thought it was,
   Because it doth endure
Vicissitude, and season, as the grasse;
Me thinkes I lyed all winter, when I swore,
My love was infinite, if spring make'it more.

But if this medicine, love, which cures all sorrow
With more, not onely bee no quintessence,
But mixt of all stuffes, paining soule, or sense,
And of the Sunne his working vigour borrow,   10
Love's not so pure, and abstract, as they use
To say, which have no Mistresse but their Muse,
But as all else, being elemented too,
Love sometimes would contemplate, sometimes do.

And yet no greater, but more eminent,
   Love by the spring is growne;
   As, in the firmament,
Starres by the Sunne are not inlarg'd, but showne.
Gentle love deeds, as blossomes on a bough,
From loves awakened root do bud out now.   20

If, as in water stir'd more circles bee
Produc'd by one, love such additions take,

Those like so many spheares, but one heaven make,
For, they are all concentrique unto thee;
And though each spring doe adde to love new heate,
As princes doe in times of action get
New taxes, and remit them not in peace,
No winter shall abate the springs encrease.

John Donne: "The Sunne Rising"

Busie old foole, unruly Sunne,
    Why dost thou thus,
Through windowes, and through curtaines call on us?
Must to thy motions lovers seasons run?
    Sawcy pedantique wretch, goe chide
    Late schoole boyes, and sowre prentices,
  Goe tell Court-huntsmen, that the King will ride,
  Call countrey ants to harvest offices;
Love, all alike, no season knowes, nor clyme,
Nor houres, dayes, moneths, which are the rags of time.

    Thy beames, so reverend, and strong   11
    Why shouldst thou thinke?
I could eclipse and cloud them with a winke,
But that I would not lose her sight so long:
    If her eyes have not blinded thine,
    Looke, and to morrow late, tell mee,
  Whether both the'India's of spice and Myne
  Be where thou leftst them, or lie here with mee.
Aske for those Kings whom thou saw'st yesterday,
And thou shalt heare, All here in one bed lay.   20

    She'is all States, and all Princes, I,
    Nothing else is.
Princes doe but play us; compar'd to this,

All honor's mimique; All wealth alchimie.
    Thou sunne art halfe as happy'as wee,
      In that the world's contracted thus;
     Thine age askes ease, and since thy duties bee
     To warme the world, that's done in warming us.
Shine here to us, and thou art every where;
This bed thy center is, these walls, thy spheare.   30

John Donne: "Elegie XII: His Parting from Her"

Since she must go, and I must mourn, come Night,
Environ me with darkness, whilst I write:
Shadow that hell unto me, which alone
I am to suffer when my Love is gone.
Alas the darkest Magick cannot do it,
Thou and greate Hell to boot are shadows to it.
Should *Cinthia* quit thee, *Venus,* and each starre,
It would not forme one thought dark as mine are.
I could lend thee obscureness now, and say,
Out of my self, There should be no more Day,   10
Such is already my felt want of sight,
Did not the fires within me force a light.
Oh Love, that fire and darkness should be mixt,
Or to thy Triumphs soe strange torments fixt?
Is't because thou thy self art blind, that wee
Thy Martyrs must no more each other see?
Or tak'st thou pride to break us on the wheel,
And view old Chaos in the Pains we feel?
Or have we left undone some mutual Right,
Through holy fear, that merits thy despight?   20
No, no. The falt was mine, impute it to me,
Or rather to conspiring destinie,
Which (since I lov'd for forme before) decreed,
That I should suffer when I lov'd indeed:
And therefore now, sooner then I can say,

I saw the golden fruit, 'tis rapt away.
Or as I had watcht one drop in a vast stream,
And I left wealthy only in a dream.
Yet Love, thou'rt blinder then thy self in this,
To vex my Dove-like friend for my amiss: 30
And, where my own sad truth may expiate
Thy wrath, to make her fortune run my fate:
So blinded Justice doth, when Favorites fall,
Strike them, their house, their friends, their followers all.
Was't not enough that thou didst dart thy fires
Into our blouds, inflaming our desires,
And made'st us sigh and glow, and pant, and burn,
And then thy self into our flame did'st turn?
Was't not enough, that thou didst hazard us
To paths in love so dark, so dangerous: 40
And those so ambush'd round with houshold spies,
And over all, thy husbands towring eyes
That flam'd with oylie sweat of jealousie:
Yet went we not still on with Constancie?
Have we not kept our guards, like spie on spie?
Had correspondence whilst the foe stood by?
Stoln (more to sweeten them) our many blisses
Of meetings, conference, embracements, kisses?
Shadow'd with negligence our most respects?
Varied our language through all dialects,   50
Of becks, winks, looks, and often under-boards
Spoak dialogues with our feet far from our words?
Have we prov'd all these secrets of our Art,
Yea, thy pale inwards, and thy panting heart?
And, after all this passed Purgatory,
Must sad divorce make us the vulgar story?
First let our eyes be rivited quite through
Our turning brains, and both our lips grow to:
Let our armes clasp like Ivy, and our fear
Freese us together, that we may stick here,   60
Till Fortune, that would rive us, with the deed

Strain her eyes open, and it make them bleed:
For Love it cannot be, whom hitherto
I have accus'd, should such a mischief doe.
Oh Fortune, thou'rt not worth my least exclame,
And plague enough thou hast in thy own shame.
Do thy great worst, my friend and I have armes,
Though not against thy strokes, against thy harmes.
Rend us in sunder, thou canst not divide
Our bodies so, but that our souls are ty'd,   70
And we can love by letters still and gifts,
And thoughts and dreams; Love never wanteth shifts.
I will not look upon the quickning Sun,
But straight her beauty to my sense shall run;
The ayre shall note her soft, the fire most pure;
Water suggest her clear, and the earth sure.
Time shall not lose our passages; the Spring
How fresh our love was in the beginning;
The Summer how it ripened in the eare;
And Autumn, what our golden harvests were.   80
The Winter I'll not think on to spite thee,
But count it a lost season, so shall shee.
And dearest Friend, since we must part, drown night
With hope of Day, burthens well born are light.
Though cold and darkness longer hang somewhere,
Yet *Phoebus* equally lights all the Sphere.
And what he cannot in like Portions pay,
The world enjoyes in Mass, and so we may.
Be then ever your self, and let no woe
Win on your health, your youth, your beauty: so   90
Declare your self base fortunes Enemy,
No less by your contempt then constancy:
That I may grow enamoured on your mind,
When my own thoughts I there reflected find.
For this to th'comfort of my Dear I vow,
My Deeds shall still be what my words are now;
The Poles shall move to teach me ere I start;

And when I change my Love, I'll change my heart;
Nay, if I wax but cold in my desire,
Think, heaven hath motion lost, and the world, fire: 100
Much more I could, but many words have made
That, oft, suspected which men would perswade;
Take therefore all in this: I love so true,
As I will never look for less in you.

John Donne: "Twicknam Garden"

Blasted with sighs, and surrounded with teares,
   Hither I come to seeke the spring,
   And at mine eyes, and at mine eares,
Receive such balmes, as else cure everything;
   But O, selfe traytor, I do bring
The spider love, which transubstantiates all,
   And can convert Manna to gall,
And that this place may thoroughly be thought
   True Paradise, I have the serpent brought.

'Twere wholsomer for mee, that winter did   10
   Benight the glory of this place,
   And that a grave frost did forbid
These trees to laugh, and mocke mee to my face;
   But that I may not this disgrace
Indure, nor yet leave loving, Love let mee
   Some senslesse peece of this place bee;
Make me a mandrake, so I may groane here,
   Or a stone fountaine weeping out my yeare.

Hither with christall vyals, lovers come,
   And take my teares, which are loves wine,   20
   And try your mistresse Teares at home,
For all are false, that tast not just like mine;
   Alas, hearts do not in eyes shine,

Nor can you more judge womans thoughts by teares,
  Then by her shadow, what she weares.
O perverse sexe, where none is true but shee,
  Who's therefore true, because her truth kills mee.

Index